Time of Grief

Mourning Poems

Also available from New Directions
edited by Jeffrey Yang

Birds, Beasts, and Seas: Nature Poems from New Directions

Time of Grief

Mourning Poems

Edited by Jeffrey Yang

A New Directions Book

For further copyright information please see Sources & Acknowledgments on p. 147.

Manufactured in the United States of America
New Directions Books are printed on acid-free paper
First published as a New Directions Paperbook Original (NDP1249) in 2013
Published simultaneously in Canada by Penguin Books Canada Limited

New Directions would like to thank Anna Steegman for originally suggesting an ND volume of mourning poems.

Library of Congress Cataloging-in-Publication Data
Time of grief: mourning poems / edited by Jeffrey Yang.
     p. cm.
  "A New Directions book."
  "New Directions Paperbook Original (NDP1249)"—T.p. verso.
  Includes index.
  ISBN 978-0-8112-2032-3 (paperbook : alk. paper)
  1. Death—Poetry. 2. Grief—Poetry. 3. Loss (Psychology)—Poetry.
  4. Bereavement—Poetry. I. Yang, Jeffrey.
  PN6110.D4T56 2013
  808.81'93548—dc23

                              2012032485

10 9 8 7 6 5 4 3 2 1

New Directions Books are published for James Laughlin
by New Directions Publishing Corporation
80 Eighth Avenue, New York, NY 10011

Out of the day and night
A joy has taken flight;
Fresh spring, and summer, and winter hoar,
Move my faint heart with grief, but with delight
No more—Oh, never more!

Percy Bysshe Shelley, from "A Lament"

"Ye shal count also to you from morrowe after the Sabbath, even
from the day that ye shal bring the sheafe of the shake offring,
seven Sabbaths, thei shalbe complete."

Leviticus 23:15 (Geneva Bible)

CONTENTS

How do we grieve? The failure of words, of life, feels most affecting in our darkest hour, and yet the voices and figures still seek us out, haunt us with memories and absence, offer no easy resolutions if any at all. Often in our disparate lives we find ourselves with no shared communal form for our grieving; often there is no time to face each inevitable season of loss (in death, in illness, suffering and fear, in love lost); often we don't know what to do because there is nothing to do. Though grief is universal, dealing with it assumes a wide array of individual and cultural-religious manifestations, which by necessity have been shaped and defined by language—prayers, chants, incantations, lamentations, poetry. For us far from the rites of tribe or clan today, it's not uncommon to find ourselves alone, bereft, forsaken in our mourning, unable to free ourselves from an endless cycle of melancholia. And yet the freedom and release we yearn for seem unattainable without mourning itself, without remembering and its obligations to live in the presence of not forgetting, "without resentment, without envy," as the poet says.

  With such thoughts in mind, this collection of poems was assembled—in the absence and the need—not as a cure for grief but as a space for mourning, for recognizing and accepting the time of grief and sharing how others have confronted it through the ages and pages of poetry. With a deepening awareness of grief's causes and convergences, perhaps readers might draw solace and strength from the lines within these leaves. We are as mortal as the earth, our dust becomes its dust. And yet, like Gotami in the *Therigatha* verses, we can be brought to madness in sorrow, walking through the secluded place of the wood, looking for a vihara sign, snowed-in vision. Gotami wandered from household to household, searching for a mustard seed that could cure her son of death. Finding none, she was cured of her madness in the realization not of impermanence, but of the impossibility of transcending social interconnectedness. She buried her son and went forth anew into the community.

  Time of Grief is divided into forty-nine days, or stations, of grief. Each day consists of a poem or a series of poems for the reader to slowly read, re-read, and dwell upon. Its structure echoes a simplified

Buddhist calendar of mourning—the forty-nine bardo days of chants and ritual meditation that assist the dead on their journey to the next life. These imperative words are spoken not only to the dead, but to the living, directed to one's self, words bearing both memento mori and the promise of rebirth.

While editing this book I discovered another 49-day period of mourning, observed in the traditional Jewish calendar, outside of the week-long shivah, between Passover and Shavuot, called the Counting of the Omer. An omer is a unit of measure equal to 5.26 U.S. pints, and according to verses in the twenty-third chapter of Leviticus, when Mosheh lead the chosen tribe into the land of Israel, an omer of the first reaping of the harvest was presented to the priest as a wave-offering to God. This waving of the grain, or *sheafe of the shake offring* in the translation of those Marian exiles in Geneva, was accompanied by meal-offerings, libations, work and food taboos, slaughtering of lambs, rams, goats, and bulls, as well as a *perfect* counting of each of the 49 days (while saving a portion of the harvest for the poor). Rabbinic commentary interprets the counting of these seven times seven Sabbaths as a mitzvah in itself, the creation of a new unit of time where time becomes an object and a blessing (for in scripture it is writ). The fulfillment of this mitzvah requires the perfect complement of 49 nights. In the early second century, the Talmud tells us, 12,000 pairs of Rabbi Akiva's students died in a plague (or battle) during the counting, and so what was originally a ritual of thanksgiving and celebration also became one of mourning.

The Counting of the Omer is practiced as a time of quiet reflection and inner growth, an accounting and taking into account, a counting upward (away from death and exile, away from the apocalyptic) to eventual atonement and renewal—*matan Torah*. Like the bardo, it forms an in-between state, an intermediary realm, a measure of time and space suspended for remembering. In the bardo the living speak to the dead and listen. The blessing is in the relation between things, their passing and recurrence. Tibetan-American poet Tsering Wangmo Dhompa writes:

> It is not out of habit
> we take flowers to the river:
> a ritual brings us closer
> to the unknown—the known,
> we guess where they go.
> Repetition (of rituals)
> wherein the hands,
> in time, cease.

Our rituals need renewal in time slowed.

    Most of the poems in this volume are published by New Directions, an independent literary press that has been publishing poetry and literature from the U.S. and beyond for over seventy-five years. The selection shifts between diverse cultures and epochs, from a mythical book of questions to the twilight of our times, though it isn't arranged chronologically but by each day's readings moved by bereavement. What the Bauhaus architects wanted is what the structure of this little anthology strives for: function clearly recognizable in the relation of forms. A pyramid of four oranges. A garland of 49 flowers, a sprig of juniper, a wave of the grain. Readers are encouraged to choose their own adventure and track down the original edition from which a compelling poem is pulled. A handful of other favorite poems are happily interwoven from the public domain. The editor would also like to point the reader to this collection's precursor volume, *Birds, Beasts, and Seas: Nature Poems from New Directions*, where some of the same poets can be found in a different field of a wholly different design, one of the pleasures of poetry being the limitless overlapping themes each poet can sing.

    Lastly, for the naming of this book I'm indebted to Gennady Aygi's collection of poetry-tributes *Time of Gratitude*, translated by Peter France. *O book / of bleeding branches*, writes Michael Palmer in a tribute to Aygi. Poetry mediates a space between grief and transformation so that the time of grief can also become a time of gratitude. For how we grieve is a part of how we live, how we envision a way to continue living when there is little more than a faltering clarity. In its lines traced through the air, in stolen scraps, on tortoise shells and tavern walls, prison walls and monuments, on silk and wood and mirrors, in the bound leaves and the burned, on the jars and bells and buried pages, in diaries of ink or light, into the caves the graves the ears…poetry lives in the echoes of the dead. Through its passages what is mourned reveals itself as flames of the spirit.

Jeffrey Yang
WINTER 2013

Time of Grief

Mourning Poems

GENNADY AYGI (1934–2006)

After Midnight – Snow Outside the Window

grief
like orphanly scattered-white clothing
(as if
of a hidden event
the fresh
departure)
to begin
and widen
through a silent land
just – everywhere – breathing desolation
the field (oh grief) with some blank spaces
(as if all is finished)
of souls

Translated from the Russian by Peter France

TOMAS TRANSTRÖMER (b. 1931)

After Someone's Death

Once there was a shock
that left behind a long pale glimmering comet's tail.
It contains us. It blurs TV images.
It deposits itself as cold drops on the aerials.

You can still shuffle along on skis in the winter sun
among groves where last year's leaves still hang.
They are like pages torn from old telephone directories—
the names are eaten up by the cold.

It is still beautiful to feel your heart throbbing.
But often the shadow feels more real than the body.
The samurai looks insignificant
beside his armor of black dragon scales.

Translated from the Swedish by Robin Fulton

CORAL BRACHO (b. 1951)

from *That Space, That Garden*

Those, the dead, they watch us with their deepened eyes,
with their inflamed hearts, and a bewilderment of children,
a desolate jolt startles us,
a private sadness.
Where?
Where did we leave behind that space?
And in their eyes, sharp and amazed, we see
that same question:
Where? Where did we leave,
where did we leave behind that space?

*

And what of that unfathomed grief,
of that sea already drained, black
among the borderless blackness?   Something fictitious
trembles, mocks itself within.

A chess piece; a perimeter.
A fissure that gasps there.
     A sham charm:
and so its absurdity, its persistence,
its abject display.   Baiting
and misleading,
     this emptiness: Nothing
could wake from it.
Only arrogance.
Only its oblique mistake.
Imperturbable.

An instant!

an instant isolated by the body's heat,
its endearing reach.

Only an instant
in the eyes, the hands!

Hushed and tenacious, the emptiness,

       —Nothing, no one
could wake from it.

     *

and its thirst.

—From there they speak to us,
from there they call to us, as between dreams

                From one dream to another

they carry us.

From one dream to another they trace us,   they transparentize us.

Like very faint traits of a landscape.
Like breath.   From one dream to another they search out
something solid: this fire
that enlaces, that endures.
This passion that takes root,
that enraptures,   and its skewed counterpoint,
this engendering feeling.   *And for your eyes it reveals
what it still reflects.*

    They join
time's light,   time's open, never-ending rooms,
its surmountable labyrinths, its embraceable coming to be:

This breathing,
this founding sap which transluces, which whelms us
like a surging wave,
like an accord: These intimate contours.

4

—A quick spinning of the crystal.   —An edge of light.

A texture.   A word.

   —Because death has rooted,
in the fertile heart of life,
its vertices,

                  and in them life burns,

in them it surrenders,   in them it joins

this thicket.

                    Translated from the Spanish by Forrest Gander

DYLAN THOMAS (1914–1953)

Grief Thief of Time

Grief thief of time crawls off,
The moon-drawn grave, with the seafaring years,
The knave of pain steals off
The sea-halved faith that blew time to his knees,
The old forget the cries,
Lean time on tide and times the wind stood rough,
Call back the castaways
Riding the sea light on a sunken path,
The old forget the grief,
Hack of the cough, the hanging albatross,
Cast back the bone of youth
And salt-eyed stumble bedward where she lies
Who tossed the high tide in a time of stories
And timelessly lies loving with the thief.

Now Jack my fathers let the time-faced crook,
Death flashing from his sleeve,
With swag of bubbles in a seedy sack
Sneak down the stallion grave,
Bull's-eye the outlaw through a eunuch crack
And free the twin-boxed grief,
No silver whistles chase him down the weeks'
Dayed peaks to day to death,
These stolen bubbles have the bites of snakes
And the undead eye-teeth,
No third eye probe into a rainbow's sex
That bridged the human halves,
All shall remain and on the graveward gulf
Shape with my fathers' thieves.

CHARLES TOMLINSON (b. 1927)

After a Death

A little ash, a painted rose, a name.
    A moonshell that the blinding sky
Puts out with winter blue, hangs
    Fragile at the edge of visibility. That space
Drawing the eye up to its sudden frontier
    Asks for a sense to read the whole
Reverted side of things. I wanted
    That height and prospect such as music brings—
Music or memory. Neither brought me here.
    This burial place straddles a green hill,
Chimneys and steeples plot the distances
    Spread vague below: only the sky
In its upper reaches keeps
    An untarnished January colour. Verse
Fronting that blaze, that blade,
    Turns to retrace the path of its dissatisfactions,
Thought coiled on thought, and only certain that
    Whatever can make bearable or bridge
The waste of air, a poem cannot.
    The husk of moon, risking the whole of space,
Seemingly sails it, frailly launched
    To its own death and fullness. We buried
A little ash. Time so broke you down,
    Your lost eyes, dry beneath
Their matted lashes, a painted rose
    Seems both to memorialize and mock
What you became. It picks your name out
    Written on the roll beside a verse—
Obstinate words: measured against the blue,
    They cannot conjure with the dead. Words,
Bringing that space to bear, that air
    Into each syllable we speak, bringing
An earnest to us of the portion
    We must inherit, what thought of that would give

The greater share of comfort, greater fear—
    To live forever, or to cease to live?
The imageless unnaming upper blue
    Defines a world, all images
Of endeavours uncompleted. Torn levels
    Of the land drop, street by street,
Pitted and pooled, its wounds
    Cleansed by a light, dealt out
With such impartiality, you'd call it kindness,
    Blindly assuaging where assuagement goes unfelt.

WILLIAM CARLOS WILLIAMS (1883–1963)

The Widow's Lament in Springtime

Sorrow is my own yard
where the new grass
flames as it has flamed
often before but not
with the cold fire
that closes round me this year.
Thirty-five years
I lived with my husband.
The plum tree is white today
with masses of flowers.
Masses of flowers
load the cherry branches
and color some bushes
yellow and some red
but the grief in my heart
is stronger than they
for though they were my joy
formerly, today I notice them
and turn away forgetting.
Today my son told me
that in the meadows,
at the edge of the heavy woods
in the distance, he saw
trees of white flowers.
I feel that I would like
to go there
and fall into those flowers
and sink into the marsh near them.

ALÍ CHUMACERO (1918–2010)

Widower's Monologue

I open the door, return to the familiar mercy
of my own house where a vague
sense protects me the son who never was
smacking of shipwreck, waves or a passionate cloak
whose acid summers
cloud the fading face. Archaic refuge
of dead gods fills the region,
and below, the wind breathes, a conscious
gust which fanned my forehead yesterday
still sought in the perturbed present.

I could not speak of sheets, candles, smoke
nor humility and compassion, calm
at the afternoon's edges, I could not
say "her hands," "her sadness," "our country"
because everything in her name
is lighted by her wounds. Like a signal sprung
of foam, an epitaph, curtains, a bed, rugs
and destruction moving toward disdain
while the lime triumphs denying her nakedness
the color of emptiness.

Now time begins, the bitter smile
of the guest who in sleeplessness sings,
waking his anger, within the vile city
the calcined music with curled lip
from indecision
that flows without cease. Star or dolphin, yonder
beneath the wave his foot vanishes,
tunics turned to emblems
sink their burning shows and with ashes
score my own forehead.

Translated from the Spanish by William Carlos Williams

INGER CHRISTENSEN (1935–2009)

from *Letter in April*

The palm tree is strong
as the wind is green.
The rage we once
called holy.
The language that once
had a direction.
The future that once
rebounded
onto us.
The indifference now
that I myself have come along
around the sun
forty-four times.
The indifference now
that the closed cycle
opens its doors.
The indifference
in this insufferable
image of reality.
Teach me to repeat
the future now,
while we are being born.
Let my mind fly up
into its nest
in the depths
of the rustling crown.
Let the eggs shine
with an afterglow
like milky sun.
Let the wind be green
and sorrow slaked.

*

A sorrow
that speaks
in clusters
of concealing
light.
So simply that light
gets the eye to see
that it is light
in the rustling
darkness.
So simply
that light is as fast
as the eye is a hole.
So easily
when the closed cycle
opens its doors,
as easily as anything,
as in the distant
acacias'
glowing
grave mounds,
the world
so killed
and buried
then and there
in light,
light
that stands still,
so easily
in April
in the April
of pain
when acacias
see me
as my mother did
when I was born.
And while I draw

and map out
whole continents
between kin
and sorrow,
the revolution turns,
hanging suspended,
and the feeling
that never leads out
is for a moment
outside
itself
and illuminated
in the dead,
inconsolable
visible
and the silence
has doors everywhere.

Translated from the Danish by Susanna Nied

GAIUS VALERIUS CATULLUS (84–54 B.C.)

Two Translations of Poem 101

Mulled hosts their countries yet mulled there by a core of wake tossed
    I've ventured these miseries, brother, our death offerings,
with the past stray more to honor my renewed remorse
    that mute and unquickened hollow queried urn, my own:
wandering when fortune ah me hid, dear, eyes you lit up—so soon,
    ah who missed her indigence brother that empty mean.
Now do mind inter here our how previous gift more our parent home
    traditional trysts tears, my renewed death offerings,
and keep here from your brother mulled many a tear he flawed to,
    of their kin perpetual, brother, ever out here fare well.

Translated from the Latin by Louis and Celia Zukofsky

*

Many the peoples many the oceans I crossed—
I arrive at these poor, brother, burials
so I could give you the last gift owed to death
and talk (why?) with mute ash.
Now that Fortune tore you from me, you
oh poor (wrongly) brother (wrongly) taken from me,
now still anyway this—what a distant mood of parents
handed down as the sad gift for burials—
accept! soaked with tears of a brother
and into forever, brother, farewell and farewell.

Translated from the Latin by Anne Carson

GU CHENG (1956–1993)

For My Grandmother, Now Departed

In the end
I understand the failings of death
so short-lived
like a whistle
the chalk lines on the playing field already faded

Yesterday, in a dream
we were assigned our house again
you paced back and forth
scuffing your feet along the floor
dropping all your belongings
into the smallest corner

Just as before, you wash clothes late into the night
humming songs as old as
the wooden washtub
and you comb your white hair
with a broken comb
just as before, when you are happy
you open the satin, fold after fold
to show me
glass buttons now disappeared
but for a lifetime you have believed
they are as beautiful as diamonds

Just as before, I want to go out
to play or go to school
outside the arched screen door
on the fifth-floor landing
lighting the stove, lightning the stove
birds are all atwitter
the whole morning
floats in light blue smoke

My life revolves around you
just as yours revolves around me

Translated from the Chinese by Joseph R. Allen

PABLO NERUDA (1904–1973)

Alberto Rojas Jiménez Comes Flying

Among frightening feathers, among nights,
among magnolias, among telegrams,
among the South wind and the maritime West,
        you come flying.

Beneath the tombs, beneath the ashes,
beneath the frozen snails,
beneath the last terrestrial waters,
        you come flying.

Farther down, among submerged girls,
and blind plants, and broken fish,
farther down, among clouds again,
        you come flying.

Beyond blood and bones,
beyond bread, beyond wine,
beyond fire,
        you come flying.

Beyond vinegar and death,
among putrefaction and violets,
with your celestial voice and your damp shoes,
        you come flying.

Over delegations and drugstores,
and wheels, and lawyers, and warships,
and red teeth recently pulled,
        you come flying.

Over sunken-roofed cities
where huge women take down their hair
with broad hands and lost combs,
        you come flying.

Next to vaults where the wine grows
with tepid turbid hands, in silence,
with slow, red-wooden hands,
          you come flying.

Among vanished aviators,
beside canals and shadows,
beside buried lilies,
          you come flying.

Among bitter-colored bottles,
among rings of anise and misfortune,
lifting your hands and weeping,
          you come flying.

Over dentists and congregations,
over moviehouses and tunnels and ears,
with a new suit and extinguished eyes,
          you come flying.

Over your wall-less cemetery,
where sailors go astray,
while the rain of your death falls,
          you come flying.

While rain of your fingers falls,
while the rain of your bones falls,
while your marrow and your laughter fall,
          you come flying.

Over the stones on which you melt,
running, down winter, down time,
while your heart descends in drops,
          you come flying.

You are not there, surrounded by cement,
and black hearts of notaries,
and infuriated riders' bones:
        you come flying.

Oh sea poppy, oh my kinsman,
oh guitar player dressed in bees,
it's not true so much shadow in your hair:
        you come flying.

It's not true so much shadow pursuing you,
it's not true so many dead swallows,
so much region dark with laments:
        you come flying.

The black wind of Valparaíso
opens its wings of coal and foam
to sweep the sky where you pass:
        you come flying.

There are ships, and a dead-sea cold,
and whistles, and months, and a smell
of rainy morning and dirty fish:
        you come flying.

There is rum, you and I, and my heart where I weep,
and nobody, and nothing, but a staircase
of broken steps, and an umbrella:
        you come flying.

There lies the sea. I go down at night and I hear you
come flying under the sea without anyone,
under the sea that dwells in me, darkened:
        you come flying.

I hear your wings and your slow flight,
and the water of the dead strikes me
like blind wet doves:
           you come flying.

You come flying, alone, solitary,
alone among the dead, forever alone,
you come flying without a shadow and without a name,
without sugar, without a mouth, without rosebushes,
           you come flying.

Translated from the Spanish by Donald D. Walsh

IZUMI SHIKIBU (ca. 970–1030)

THREE POEMS

I.
At the Sutra chanting of her dead daughter

In love longing
I listen to the monk's bell.
I will never forget you
even for an interval
short as those between the bell notes.

II.

Soon I shall cease to be.
When I am beyond this world,
can I have the memory
of just one more meeting?

III.

Out of the darkness
on a dark path,
I now set out.
Shine on me,
moon of the mountain edge.

Translated by Kenneth Rexroth and Ikuko Atsumi

FORREST GANDER (b. 1956)

TWO POEMS

Meditative

Out from the ordeal
came silence.
Substituted for intention,
thunderstruck by a tongue.
Otherwordly relief

abolishes sthenic sobbing,
rhythmic heaves, wind-whipped
funeral banners. All the less
strange since it is death
who constructs silence,
who climbs into silence
by her longish hair.

Poem

Some
we say we
know go
like a window
dark.
Pathetic
any remark
then.
They leave
us, what
we call
them.

KAZUKO SHIRAISHI (b. 1931)

Sumiko's Summertime

summertime is   birthday   Sumiko's
Sumiko's birthday   tiny   as a gecko
with cute cheeks   Sumiko used magic
pretended to be old   in the blink of an eye
with a slightly sad expression   she began to bake
the bread of loneliness in her oven   but the guests
who had come to eat   one by one
deer   fox   hares   badgers   and birds   and young girls and boys
all   disappeared   and these woods are *empty*
the woods   and the magic disappeared   Sumiko   is sixteen
     again
the young girl   Sumiko   today is her birthday
summertime is   everyday   everyday   a birthday
even when we ask   where's Sumiko?
she just giggles   in a little   cute voice
up above the white clouds   under the desk   beyond the door
playing hide-and-seek   she doesn't come out   doesn't come out
summertime is   birthday   Sumiko's   Sumiko's
birthday   toward morning   a thunderclap   the angels are
     surprised
tiny   as a gecko
with cute cheeks   Sumiko   puts eternity
into a spoon   and relishes eating it
is it "delicious   as love"?
the taste of honey   summertime   invisible Sumiko's
birthday   a sixteen-year-old   girl   Sumiko   playing
     hide-and-seek
even when we call   you can come out now   she
     doesn't come out

she doesn't intend to come out   ever
summertime is   in high spirits   sobbing and sobbing
today is Sumiko's birthday   Sumiko's   Sumiko's birthday

Translated from the Japanese by
Yumiko Tsumura and Samuel Grolmes

WILLIAM BRONK (1918–1999)

The Arts and Death: A Fugue for Sidney Cox

I think always how we always miss it. Not
anything is ever entirely true.

Death dominates my mind. I
do not stop thinking how time will stop,
how time has stopped, does stop. Those dead—
their done time. Time does us in.

Mark how we make music, images,
how we term words, name names,
how, having named, assume the named begins
here, stops there, add this attribute,
subtract this other: here the mold begins
to harden. This toy soldier has
edges, can be painted, picked up,
moved from place to place, used to mean
one or many. Within the game we play,
we understand. See his leaden gun
or saber, how deadly for aid or for
destruction as we aim him, and he is bold,
a game soldier. We play games
however serious we aim to be.
A true aim, a toy soldier. I think
always, how we always miss the aim.

Ponder the vast debris of the dead, the great
uncounted numbers, the long, the endless list
of only their names, if anyone knew their names.
Joined to the dead already, to those known
who have died already, are we not also joined
to many we would have known in their time—
to one in Ilium, say, who thought of the dead?
In the world's long continuum, it is not
the names of the dead, but the dead themselves who are like
names, like terms, toy soldiers, words.

I think always how we always miss it; how the dead
have not been final, and life has always required
to be stated again, which is not ever stated.
It is not art's statements only, not
what we try to say by music, not the way
this picture sculptures sight itself
to see this picture—not by art alone
the aim is missed, and even least of all
by art (which tries a whole world at once,
a composition). No, it is in our terms,
the terms themselves, which break apart, divide,
discriminate, set chasms in that wide,
unbroken experience of the senses which
goes on and on, that radiation, inward and out,
that consciousness which we divide, compare,
compose, make things and persons of, make forms,
make I and you. World, world, I am scared
and waver in awe before the wilderness
of raw consciousness, because it is all
dark and formlessness; and it is real
this passion that we feel for forms. But the forms
are never real. Are not really there. Are not.

I think always how we always miss the real.

There still are wars though all the soldiers fall.

We live in a world we never understand.

Our lives end nothing. Oh there is never an end.

ROBERT CREELEY (1926–2005)

Mitch

Mitch was a classmate
later married extraordinary poet
and so our families were friends
when we were all young
and lived in New York, New Hampshire, France.

He had eyes with whites
above eyeballs looked out
over lids in droll surmise—
"gone under earth's lid" was Pound's phrase,
cancered stomach?

A whispered information over phone,
two friends the past week…,
the one, she says, an eccentric dear woman,
conflicted with son?
Convicted with ground

tossed in, one supposes,
more dead than alive.
Life's done all it could
for all of them.
Time to be gone?

Not since 1944–45
have I felt so dumbly, utterly,
in the wrong place at
entirely the wrong time,
caught then in that merciless war,

now trapped here, old, on a blossoming earth,
nose filled with burgeoning odors,
wind a caress, sound blurred reassurance,
echo of others, the lovely compacting
human warmths, the eye closing upon you,

seeing eye, sight's companion, dark or light,
makes out of its lonely distortions
it's you again, coming closer, feel
weight in the bed beside me,
close to my bones.

They told me it would be
like this but who could
believe it, not to leave, not to
go away? "I'll hate to
leave this earthly paradise…"

There's no time like the present,
no time in the present. Now it floats, goes out like a boat
upon the sea. Can't we see,
can't we now be company
to that one of us

has to go? *Hold my hand, dear.*
I should have hugged him,
taken him up, held him,
in my arms. I should
have let him know I was here.

Is it my turn now,
who's to say or wants to?
You're not sick, there are
certainly those older.
Your time will come.

In God's hands it's cold.
In the universe it's an empty, echoing silence.
Only us to make sounds,
but I made none.
I sat there like a stone.

WILLIAM WORDSWORTH (1770–1850)

"When, to the attractions of the busy world"

When, to the attractions of the busy world
Preferring studious leisure, I had chosen
A habitation in this peaceful Vale,
Sharp season followed of continual storm
In deepest winter; and, from week to week,
Pathway, and lane, and public road, were clogged
With frequent showers of snow. Upon a hill
At a short distance from my cottage, stands
A stately Fir-grove, whither I was wont
To hasten, for I found, beneath the roof
Of that perennial shade, a cloistral place
Of refuge, with an unencumbered floor.
Here, in safe covert, on the shallow snow,
And sometimes on a speck of visible earth,
The redbreast near me hopped; nor was I loth
To sympathize with vulgar coppice birds
That, for protection from the nipping blast,
Hither repaired.—A single beech-tree grew
Within this grove of firs! and, on the fork
Of that one beech, appeared a thrush's nest;
A last year's nest, conspicuously built
At such small elevation from the ground
As gave sure sign that they, who in that house
Of nature and of love had made their home
Amid the fir-trees, all the summer long
Dwelt in a tranquil spot. And oftentimes
A few sheep, stragglers from some mountain-flock,
Would watch my motions with suspicious stare,
From the remotest outskirts of the grove,—
Some nook where they had made their final stand,
Huddling together from two fears—the fear
Of me and of the storm. Full many an hour
Here did I lose. But in this grove the trees
Had been so thickly planted and had thriven

In such perplexed and intricate array,
That vainly did I seek beneath their stems
A length of open space, where to and fro
My feet might move without concern or care;
And, baffled thus, though earth from day to day
Was fettered, and the air by storm disturbed,
I ceased the shelter to frequent,—and prized,
Less than I wished to prize, that calm recess.

The snows dissolved, and genial Spring returned
To clothe the fields with verdure. Other haunts
Meanwhile were mine; till one bright April day,
By chance retiring from the glare of noon
To this forsaken covert, there I found
A hoary pathway traced between the trees,
And winding on with such an easy line
Along a natural opening, that I stood
Much wondering how I could have sought in vain For what was
now so obvious. To abide,
For an allotted interval of ease,
Under my cottage-roof, had gladly come
From the wild sea a cherished Visitant;
And with the sight of this same path—begun,
Begun and ended, in the shady grove,
Pleasant conviction flashed upon my mind
That, to this opportune recess allured,
He had surveyed it with a finer eye,
A heart more wakeful; and had worn the track
By pacing here, unwearied and alone,
In that habitual restlessness of foot
That haunts the Sailor, measuring o'er and o'er
His short domain upon the vessel's deck,
While she pursues her course through the dreary sea.

When thou hadst quitted Eathwaite's pleasant shore,
And taken thy first leave of those green hills
And rocks that were the play-ground of thy youth,

Year followed year, my Brother! and we two,
Conversing not, knew little in what mould
Each other's mind was fashioned; and at length,
When once again we met in Grasmere Vale,
Between us there was little other bond
Than common feelings of fraternal love.
But thou, a School-boy, to the sea hadst carried
Undying recollections; Nature there
Was with thee; she, who loved us both, she still
Was with thee; and even so didst thou become
A *silent* Poet; from the solitude
Of the vast sea didst bring a watchful heart
Still couchant, an inevitable ear,
And an eye practised like a blind man's touch.
—Back to the joyless Ocean thou art gone;
Nor from this vestige of thy musing hours
Could I withhold thy honoured name,—and now
I love the fir-grove with a perfect love.
Thither do I withdraw when cloudless suns
Shine hot, or wind blows troublesome and strong;
And there I sit at evening, when the steep
Of Silver-how, and Grasmere's peaceful lake
And one green island, gleam between the stems
Of the dark firs, a visionary scene!
And while I gaze upon the spectacle
Of clouded splendour, on this dream-like sight
Of solemn loveliness, I think on thee,
My brother, and on all which thou has lost.
Nor seldom, if I rightly guess, while Thou,
Muttering the verses which I muttered first
Among the mountains, through the midnight watch
Art pacing thoughtfully the vessel's deck
In some far region, here, while o'er my head,
At every impulse of the moving breeze,
The fir-grove murmurs with a sea-like sound,
Alone I tread this path;—for aught I know,
Timing my steps to thine; and, with a store

Of undistinguishable sympathies,
Mingling most earnest wishes for the day
When we, and others whom we love, shall meet
A second time, in Grasmere's happy Vale.

SOPHOKLES (496–406 B.C.)

from *Women of Trachis*

Ant. 2   LET the tears flow.
Ne'er had bright Herakles in his shining
Need of pity till now
     […]

KHOROS (*declaimed*):

Str. 1   TORN between griefs, which grief shall I lament,
which first? Which last, in heavy argument?
One wretchedness to me in double load.

Ant. 1   DEATH'S in the house,
     and death comes by the road.

(sung)
Str. 2   That wind might bear away my grief and me,
Sprung from the hearth-stone, let it bear me away.
God's Son is dead,
    that was so brave and strong,
And I am craven to behold such death
    Swift on the eye,
Pain hard to uproot,
    and this so vast
A splendour of ruin.

Ant. 2   THAT NOW is here.
As Progne shrill upon the weeping air,
'tis no great sound.
    These strangers lift him home,
with shuffling feet, and love that keeps them still.
The great weight silent
    for no man can say
If sleep but feign
    or Death reign instantly.

HERAKLES (*in the mask of divine agony*):

> Brother of God, Sweet Hell, be decent.
> Let me lie down and rest.
> Swift-feathered Death, that art the end of shame.
>   [...]
> Misery. I'm going out
> and my light's gone.
> The black out!
> I understand perfectly well
> where things have got to...
>   [...]
> Time lives, and it's going on now.
> I am released from trouble.
> I thought it meant life in comfort.
> It doesn't. It means that I die.
> For amid the dead there is no work in service.
> Come at it that way, my boy, what

SPLENDOUR,
>   IT ALL COHERES.

Translated from the Greek by Ezra Pound

from *Antigonick*

ANTIGONE: O tomb O bridal chamber O house in the ground forever I was an organized person and this is my reward I organized your deaths dear ones all of you father mother brother when you died you ask would I have done it for a husband or a child my answer is No I would not. A husband or a child can be replaced but who can grow me a new brother is this a weird argument, Kreon thought so but I don't know, the words go wrong they call my piety impiety, I'm alone on my insides I died long ago. Who suffers more I wonder who suffers more

CHORUS: Your soul is blowing Apart

Translated from the Greek by Anne Carson

BASIL BUNTING (1900–1985)

A Song for Rustam

Tears are for what can be mended,
not for a voyage ended
the day the schooner put out.
Short fear and sudden quiet
too deep for a diving thief.
Tears are for easy grief.

My soil is shorn,
forests and corn.
Winter will bare the rock.
What has he left of pride
whose son is dead?
My soil has shaved its head.

The sky withers and stinks.
Star after star sinks
into the west, by you.
Whirling, spokes of the wheel
hoist up a faded day,
its sky wrinkled and grey.

Words slung to the gale
stammer and fail:
'Unseen is not unknown,
unkissed is not unloved,
unheard is not unsung;'
Words late, lost, dumb.

Truth that shone is dim,
lies cripple every limb.
Where you were, you are not.
Silent, heavy air
stifles the heart's leap.
Truth is asleep.

DOROTHY WELLESLEY (1889–1956)

The Buried Child
EPILOGUE TO "DESERTED HOUSE"

He is not dead nor liveth
The little child in the grave,
And men have known for ever
That he walketh again;
They hear him November evenings,
When acorns fall with the rain.

Deep in the hearts of men
Within his tomb he lieth,
And when the heart is desolate
He desolate sigheth.

Teach me then the heart of the dead child,
Who, holding a tulip, goeth
Up the stairs in his little grave-shift,
Sitting down in his little chair
By his biscuit and orange,
In the nursery he knoweth.

Teach me all that the child who knew life
And the quiet of death,
To the croon of the cradle-song
By his brother's crib
In the deeps of the nursery dusk
To his mother saith.

STÉPHANE MALLARMÉ (1842–1898)

from *A Tomb for Anatole*

1
child sprung from
the two of us — showing
us our ideal, the way
— ours! father
and mother who
        sadly existing
survive him as
the two extremes —
badly coupled in him
and sundered
— from whence his death — o-
bliterating this little child "self"

7
            what has taken refuge
your future   in me
        becomes my
purity through life,
which I shall not
    touch —

21
⌈sick — to be naked
⌊like the child —

and appearing before us
— we take advantage of these
hours, when death
                struck down
he lives

      again, and
  again is ours

title poetry of
      the sickness.

37
time of the
    empty room
—

    until we
        open it
perhaps all
      follows from this
      (morally)
     ———

46
    no — nothing
  to do with the great
  deaths — etc.
  — as long as we
  go on living, he
  lives — in us
—

it will only be after our
death that he will be dead
— and the bells
of the Dead will toll for
            him

61
death — whispers softly
  — I am no one —
    I do not even know who I am
    (for the dead do not
    know they are
    dead —, nor even that they
                              die
    — for children
    at least
            — or

76
family perfect
balance
    father son
    mother daughter

broken —
three, a void
among us,
          searching...

79
no more life for

        —

me
    and I feel
I am lying in the grave
beside you.

81
  death
  there are only conso-
lations, thoughts — balm

  but what is done
is done — we cannot
hark back to the absolute stuff of death —

  — and nevertheless
to show that if,
once life has been

126
  cemetery
  the need to go there
  to renew
        laceration
  pain — through
            the dear being
  idea of <death> there

———

  when the too powerful
  illusion of having him
  always with us

no, you are not one of the dead
— you will not be among
the dead, always in us

177
>   to close his eyes
— I do not want
to close his eyes —
>   — that will look
>   at me always

_____

 or death aside

_____

>   closed eyes, etc.
 we see him again in sickness
struggling against this horrible
state —

183
true mourning in
 the apartment
— not cemetery —

>   furniture

185
>   little sailor —
sailor suit
>   what!
— for enormous
>   crossing
a wave will carry you
>   ascetic
>   sea,

>   < + + >

187
know that he is no longer
here

and if, he is there — absent —
from which mother herself
has become phantom —
spiritualized by
habit of living
with a vision

Translated from the French by Paul Auster

DENISE LEVERTOV (1923–1997)

At David's Grave
FOR B. AND H. F.

Yes, he is here in this
open field, in sunlight, among
the few young trees set out
to modify the bare facts—

he's here, but only
because we are here.
When we go, he goes with us

to be your hands that never
do violence, your eyes
that wonder, your lives

that daily praise life
by living it, by laughter.

He is never alone here,
never cold in the field of graves.

JOHANNES BOBROWSKI (1917–1965)

Silcher's Grave

At one side, the bench in front of the wall,
in the leafy shadow, cross and small tree
above the grave: in the long silence
which began after the songs of friendship

and outsang time and name. There is a residue
of dead voices, hands, as though fallen
unopened into the lap. No question
more to be heard, none answered.

Translated from the German by Ruth and Matthew Mead

STEVIE SMITH (1902–1971)

Grave by a Holm-Oak

You lie there, Anna,
In your grave now,
Under a snow-sky,
You lie there now.

Where have the dead gone?
Where do they live now?
Not in the grave, they say,
Then where now?

Tell me, tell me,
Is it where I may go?
Ask not, cries the holm-oak,
Weep, says snow.

NICANOR PARRA (b. 1914)

Rest in Peace

sure—rest in peace
but what about the damp?
        and the moss?
                and the weight of the tombstone?
and the drunken gravediggers?
and the people who steal the flowerpots?
and the rats gnawing at the coffins?
and the damned worms
crawling in everywhere
they make death impossible for us
or do you really think
we don't know what's going on…

fine for you to say rest in peace
when you know damn well that's impossible
you just like running off at the mouth

well for your information
we know what's going on
the spiders scurrying up our legs
make damn sure of that

let's cut the crap
when you stand at a wide open grave
it's time to call a spade a spade:
You can drown your sorrows at the wake
we're stuck at the bottom of the pit.

Translated from the Spanish by Edith Grossman

ROBERTO BOLAÑO (1953–2003)

from *A Stroll Through Literature*

2. We're underdone, father, not cooked or raw, lost in the vastness of this endless dump, wandering and going astray, killing and asking forgiveness, manic depressives in your dream, father, your dream that had no borders and that we've disemboweled a thousand times and then a thousand more, like Latin American detectives lost in a labyrinth of crystal and mud, traveling in the rain, seeing movies where old men appear screaming *tornado! tornado!*, watching things for the last time, but without seeing them, like specters, like frogs at the bottom of a well, father, lost in the misery of your utopian dream, lost in the variety of your voices and your abysses, manic depressives in the boundless room of Hell where your Humor cooks.

4. In these ruins, father, where archeological remains are all that's left of your laughter.

11. I dreamt that in a forgotten African cemetery I came across the tomb of a friend whose face I could no longer remember.

17. I dreamt I was an old, sick detective and I was looking for people lost long ago. Sometimes I'd look at myself casually in a mirror and recognize Roberto Bolaño.

26. I dreamt I was fifteen and was going to Nicanor Parra's house to say goodbye. I found him standing, leaning against a black wall. Where are you going, Bolaño? he said. Far from the Southern Hemisphere, I answered.

41. I dreamt I was dreaming and in the dream tunnels I found Roque Dalton's dream: the dream of the brave ones who died for a fucking chimera.

53. I dreamt I went back to the streets, but this time I wasn't fifteen but over forty. All I had was a book, which I carried in my tiny backpack. At once, while I was walking, the book started to burn. It was getting light out and hardly any cars passed. When I chucked my scorched backpack into a ditch my back was stinging as if I had wings.

Translated from the Spanish by Laura Healy

LULJETA LLESHANAKU (b. 1968)

Chess

Autumn. Veins of marble
swell in the rain.

The graves of my relatives
four inches of space between them
lined up
like cars at a railroad crossing.

What once kept them together
like fingers in an ironsmith's glove
has vanished…. The war is over.

In the afterlife there are only a few strangers
waiting for the train to pass…

The smell of the earth
reminds me of home
where a clock that once hung on the wall is missing.

I polish the dust off their names with care—
the years… like little bruises on a knee,
love… which now pricks less
than the thorns of a rose.

There, at the entrance to the cemetery
the guard sits in his booth
playing chess with himself.

Translated from the Albanian by Henry Israeli and Shpresa Qatipi

FEDERICO GARCÍA LORCA (1898–1936)

from *Lament for Ignacio Sánchez Mejías*

ABSENT SOUL

The bull does not know you, nor the fig tree,
nor the horses, nor the ants in your own house.
The child and the afternoon do not know you
because you have died for ever.

The back of the stone does not know you,
nor the black satin in which you crumble.
Your silent memory does not know you
because you have died for ever.

The autumn will come with small white snails,
misty grapes and with clustered hills,
but no one will look into your eyes
because you have died for ever.

Because you have died for ever,
like all the dead of the Earth,
like all the dead who are forgotten
in a heap of lifeless dogs.

Nobody knows you. No. But I sing of you.
For posterity I sing of your profile and grace.
Of the signal maturity of your understanding.
Of your appetite for death and the taste of its mouth.
Of the sadness of your once valiant gaiety.

It will be a long time, if ever, before there is born
an Andalusian so true, so rich in adventure.
I sing of his elegance with words that groan,
and I remember a sad breeze through the olive trees.

Translated from the Spanish by Stephen Spender and J. L. Gili

LAWRENCE FERLINGHETTI (b. 1919)

Allen Still

Allen died 49 nights ago, and in Bixby Canyon now the white misshapen moon sailed listing through the sky all night across the horizon above this bowl of hills followed by a white star, no fog in the morning, bright and clear, warm air for this hour, birds up early telling their night's stories always different always the same, so few notes to tell the tale, just before first light, moon fading on western rim of canyon, the following star washed out by sun's first lighting, willows and yellow lupin and yellow mustard blossoms and cactus and bell-shaped white morning glory reaching up silent exulting (We are alive and breathing!) the woods full of tiny life teeming, tiny lives chirring in the dense green, under the lush willows, beeches and dying alders.... Lorenzo and lady still asleep, she two months pregnant (conceived perhaps the night Allen died)... he pregnant in the earth now though cremated and buddhist spirit exited through top of head, his burnt dust now feeding some other embryo bird or frog....What will arise from it, from him, dusty *passageur*?

MARINA TSVETAEVA (1892–1941)

Wires

TO BORIS PASTERNAK

To tell you everything… But no, all cramped
In rows and rhymes… Wider the heart!
For such a disaster I fear that all
Racine and Shakespeare would fall short.

"All wept, and if the blood is aching…
All wept, and if the roses conceal snakes…"
But Phaedra had only one Hippolytus,
And Ariadne's tears were for one Theseus.

Excruciation! Without shore or limit!
Yes, I lose track of figures and declare
That when I lose you, I lose everyone
Who never was in any time or anywhere.

What can I hope—when riddled through and through
With you the whole air has grown one with me!
When every bone to me is like a Naxos!
When the blood under my skin is like the Styx!

In vain! Within me! Everywhere! I close
My eyes: it is dateless, bottomless.
The calendar lies ….
                    As you are the Break,
So I am not Ariadne, not….
                    —I am Loss.

O through what seas and towns shall I
Search for you? (The unseeing for the unseen!)
I trust my farewells to the telegraph wires
And pressed against a telegraph pole—I weep.

Translated from the Russian by Peter France

EMILY BRONTË (1818–1848)

Sympathy

There should be no despair for you
    While nightly stars are burning;
While evening pours its silent dew,
    And sunshine gilds the morning.
There should be no despair—though tears
    May flow down like a river:
Are not the best beloved of years
    Around your heart for ever?

They weep, you weep, it must be so;
    Winds sigh as you are sighing,
And winter sheds its grief in snow
    Where Autumn's leaves are lying:
Yet, these revive, and from their fate
    Your fate cannot be parted:
Then, journey on, if not elate,
    Still, *never* broken-hearted!

RAINER MARIA RILKE (1875–1926)

Requiem For a Friend

I have my dead, and I would let them go
and be surprised to see them all so cheerful,
so soon at home in being-dead, so right,
so unlike their repute. You, you alone,
return; brush past me, move about, persist
in knocking something that vibratingly
betrays you. Oh, don't take from me what I
am slowly learning. I'm right; you're mistaken,
if you're disturbed into a home-sick longing
for something here. We transmute it all;
it's not here, we reflect it from ourselves,
from our own being, as soon as we perceive it.

I thought you'd got much further. It confounds me
that *you* should thus mistake and come, who passed
all other women so in transmutation.
That we were frightened when you died, or, rather,
that your strong death made a dark interruption,
tearing the till-then from the ever-since:
that is our business: to set that in order
will be the work that everything provides us.
But that you too were frightened, even now
are frightened, now, when fright has lost its meaning,
that you are losing some of your eternity,
even a little, to step in here, friend, here,
where nothing yet exists; that in the All,
for the first time distracted and half-hearted,
you did not grasp the infinite ascension
as once you grasped each single thing on earth,
that from the orbit that already held you
the gravitation of some mute unrest
should drag you down to measurable time:
this often wakes me like an entering thief.
If I could say you merely deign to come
from magnanimity, from superabundance,

because you are so sure, so self-possessed,
that you can wander like a child, not frightened
of places where ther're things that happen to one—
but no, you're asking. And that penetrates
right to the bone and rattles like a saw.
Reproach, such as you might bear as a spirit,
bear against me when I withdraw myself
at night into my lungs, into my bowels,
into the last poor chamber of my heart,
such a reproach would not be half so cruel
as this mute asking. What is it you ask?

Say, shall I travel? Have you left somewhere
a thing behind you, that torments itself
with trying to reach you? Travel to a country
you never saw, although it was as closely
akin to you as one half of your senses?

I'll voyage on its rivers, set my foot
upon its soil and ask about old customs,
stand talking with the women in their doorways
and pay attention when they call their children.
I will observe how they take on the landscape
outside there in the course of the old labor
of field and meadow; will express a wish
to be presented to the king himself,
and work upon the priests with bribery
to leave me lying before the strongest statue
and then withdraw, shutting the temple doors.
But in conclusion, having learnt so much,
I'll simply watch the animals, that something
of their own way of turning may glide over
into my joints; I'll have a brief existence
within their eyes, that solemnly retain me
and slowly loose me, calmly, without judgment.
I'll make the gardeners repeat by heart
the names of many flowers and so bring back
in pots of lovely proper names a remnant,
a little remnant, of the hundred perfumes.

And I will purchase fruits too, fruits, wherein
that country, sky and all, will re-exist.

For that was what you understood: full fruits.
You used to set them out in bowls before you
and counterpoise their heaviness with colors.
And women too appeared to you as fruits,
and children too, both of them from within
impelled into the forms of their existence.
And finally you say yourself as fruit,
lifted yourself out of your clothes and carried
that self before the mirror, let it in
up to your gaze; which remained, large, in front,
and did not say: that's me; no, but: this is.
So uninquiring was your gaze at last,
so unpossesive and so truly poor,
it wanted even you no longer: holy.

That's how I would retain you, as you placed
yourself within the mirror, deep within,
and far from all else. Why come differently?
Why thus revoke yourself? Why are you trying
to make me feel that in those amber beads
around your neck there was still something heavy
with such a heaviness as never lurks
in the beyond of tranquil pictures? Why
does something in your bearing bode misfortune?
What makes you read the contours of your body
like lines upon a hand, and me no longer
able to see them but as destiny?

Come to the candle-light. I'm not afraid
to look upon the dead. When they return
they have a right to hospitality
within our gaze, the same as other things.

Come; we'll remain a little while in silence.
Look at this rose, here on my writing-desk:
is not the light around it just as timid
as that round you? It too should not be here.
It ought to have remained or passed away

out in the garden there, unmixed with me—
it stays, unconscious of my consciousness.

Don't be afraid now if I comprehend:
it's rising in me—oh, I must, I must,
even if it kills me, I must comprehend.
Comprehend, that you're here. I comprehend.
Just as a blind man comprehends a thing,
I feel your fate although I cannot name it.
Let both of us lament that someone took you
out of your mirror. If you still can cry?
No, you can't cry. You long ago transformed
the force and thrust of tears to your ripe gazing,
and were in act of changing every kind
of sap within you to a strong existence
that mounts and circles in blind equipoise.
Then, for the last time, chance got hold of you,
and snatched you back out of your farthest progress,
back to a world where saps will have their way.
Did not snatch all, only a piece at first,
but when reality, from day to day,
so swelled around that piece that it grew heavy,
you needed your whole self; then off you went
and broke yourself in fragments from your law,
laboriously, needing yourself. And then
you took yourself away and from your heart's
warm, night-warm, soil you dug the yet green seeds
your death was going to spring from: your own death,
the death appropriate to your own life.
And then you ate those grains of your own death
like any others, ate them one by one,
and had within yourself an after-taste
of unexpected sweetness, had sweet lips,
you: in your senses sweet within already.

   Let us lament. Do you know how unwilling
and hesitatingly your blood returned,

recalled from an incomparable orbit?
With what confusion it took up again
the tiny circulation of the body?
With what mistrust it entered the placenta,
suddenly tired from the long homeward journey?
You drove it on again, you pushed it forward,
you dragged it to the hearth, as people drag
a herd of animals to sacrifice;
and in spite of all desired it to be happy.
And finally you forced it: it was happy,
and ran up and surrendered. You supposed,
being so accustomed to the other measures,
that this was only for a little while;
but now you were in time, and time is long.
And time goes by, and time goes on, and time
is like relapsing after some long illness.

How very short your life, when you compare it
with hours you used to sit in silence, bending
the boundless forces of your boundless future
out of their course to the new germination,
that became fate once more. O painful labor.
Labor beyond all strength. And you performed it
day after day, you dragged yourself along to it
and pulled the lovely woof out of the loom
and wove your threads into another pattern.
And still had spirit for a festival.

For when you'd done you looked for some reward,
like children, when they've drunk a nasty drink
of bitter-sweet tea that may make one better.
You gave your own reward, being still so distant,
even then, from all the rest; and no one there
who could have hit on a reward to please you.
You yourself knew it. You sat up in child-bed,
a mirror there before you, that returned
all that you gave. Now everything was you,
and right in front; within was mere deceit,

the sweet deceit of Everywoman, gladly
putting her jewels on and doing her hair.

And so you died like women long ago,
died in the old warm house, old-fashionedly,
the death of those in child-bed, who are trying
to close themselves again but cannot do it,
because that darkness which they also bore
returns and grows importunate and enters.

Ought they not, though, to have gone and hunted up
some mourners for you? Women who will weep
for money, and, if paid sufficiently,
will howl through a whole night when all is still.
Observances! We have not enough
observances. All vanishes in talk.
That's why you have to come back, and with me
retrieve omitted mourning. Can you hear me?
I'd like to fling my voice out like a cloth
over the broken fragments of your death
and tug at it till it was all in tatters,
and everything I said was forced to go
clad in the rags of that torn voice and freeze—
if mourning were enough. But I accuse:
not him who thus withdrew you from yourself
(I can't distinguish him, he's like them all),
but in him I accuse all: accuse man.

If somewhere deep within me rises up
a having-once-been-child I don't yet know,
perhaps the purest childness of my childhood:
I will not know it. Without looking at it
or asking, I will make an angel of it,
and hurl that angel to the foremost rank
of crying angels that remembrance God.

For now too long this suffering has lasted,
and none can stand it; it's too hard for us,
this tortuous suffering caused by spurious love,

which, building on prescription like a habit,
calls itself just and battens on injustice.
Where is the man who justly may possess?
Who can possess what cannot hold itself
but only now and then blissfully catches
and flings itself on like a child a ball?
As little as the admiral can retain
the Nikê poised upon his vessel's prow
when the mysterious lightness of her godhead
has caught her up into the limpid sea-wind,
can one of us call back to him the woman
who, seeing us no longer, takes her way
along some narrow strip of her existence,
as though a miracle, without mischance—
unless his calling and delight were guilt.

   For this is guilt, if anything be guilt,
not to enlarge the freedom of a love
with all the freedom in one's own possession.
All we can offer where we love is this:
to loose each other; for to hold each other
comes easy to us and requires no learning.

Are you still there? Still hiding in some corner?—
You knew so much of all that I've been saying,
and could know so much, for you passed through life
open to all things, like a breaking day.
Women suffer: loving means being lonely,
and artists feel at times within their work
the need, where most they love, for transmutation.
You began both; and both exist in *that*
which fame, detaching it from you, disfigures.
Oh, you were far beyond all fame. Were in-
conspicuous; had gently taken in
your beauty as a gala flag's intaken
on the grey morning of a working-day,
and wanted nothing but a lengthy work—
which is not done; in spite of all, not done.

If you're still there, if somewhere in this darkness
there's still a spot where your perceptive spirit's
vibrating on the shallow waves of sound
a lonely voice within a lonely night
starts in the air-stream of a lofty room:
hear me and help me. Look, without knowing when,
we keep on slipping backwards from our progress
into some unintended thing, and there
we get ourselves involved as in a dream,
and there at last we die without awakening.
No one's got further. Anyone who's lifted
the level of his blood to some long work
may find he's holding it aloft no longer
and that it's worthlessly obeying its weight.
For somewhere there's an old hostility
between our human life and greatest work.
May I see into it and it say: help me!

Do not return. If you can bear it, stay
dead with the dead. The dead are occupied.
But help me, as you may without distraction,
as the most distant sometimes helps: in me.

Translated from the German by J. B. Leishman

AHARON SHABTAI (b. 1939)

My Heart's as Empty as this Pail

My heart's as empty as this pail
without you

I'll lean
over the bathtub
and fill it with water

and soak
the washrag in it

then mop the floor

Translated from the Hebrew by Peter Cole

GIACOMO LEOPARDI (1798–1837)

Her Monument, the Image Cut Thereon

Such wast thou,
Who art now
But buried dust and rusted skeleton.
Above the bones and mire,
Motionless, placed in vain,
Mute mirror of the flight of speeding years,
Sole guard of grief
Sole guard of memory
Standeth this image of the beauty sped.

O glance, when thou wast still as thou art now,
How hast thou set the fire
A-tremble in men's veins; O lip curved high
To mind me of some urn of full delight,
O throat girt round of old with swift desire,
O palms of Love, that in your wonted ways
Not once but many a day
Felt hands turn ice a-sudden, touching ye,
That ye were once! of all the grace ye had
That which remaineth now
Shameful, most sad
Find 'neath this rock fit mould, fit resting place!

And still when fate recalleth,
Even that semblance that appears amongst us
Is like to heaven's most 'live imagining.
All, all our life's eternal mystery!

To-day, on high
Mounts, from our mighty thoughts and from the fount
Of sense untellable, Beauty
That seems to be some quivering splendor cast
By the immortal nature on this quicksand,
And by surhuman fates

Given to mortal state
To be a sign and an hope made secure
Of blissful kingdoms and the aureate spheres;
And on the morrow, by some lightsome twist,
Shameful in sight, abject, abominable
All this angelic aspect can return
And be but what it was
With all the admirable concepts that moved from it
Swept from the mind with it in its departure.

Infinite things desired, lofty visions
'Got on desirous thought by natural virtue,
And the wise concord, whence through delicious seas
The arcane spirit of the whole Mankind
Turns hardy pilot... and if one wrong note
Strike the tympanum,
Instantly
That paradise is hurled to nothingness.

O mortal nature,
If thou art
Frail and so vile in all,
How canst thou reach so high with thy poor sense;
Yet if thou art
Noble in any part
How is the noblest of thy speech and thought
So lightly wrought
Or to such base occasion lit and quenched?

Translated from the Italian by Ezra Pound

KENNETH REXROTH (1905–1982)

Andree Rexroth

MT. TAMALPAIS

The years have gone. It is spring
Again. Mars and Saturn will
Soon come on, low in the West,
In the dusk. Now the evening
Sunlight makes hazy girders
Over Steep Ravine above
The waterfalls. The winter
Birds from Oregon, robins
And varied thrushes, feast on
Ripe toyon and madroñe
Berries. The robins sing as
The dense light falls.
                              Your ashes
Were scattered in this place. Here
I wrote you a farewell poem,
And long ago another,
A poem of peace and love,
Of the lassitude of a long
Spring evening in youth. Now
It is almost ten years since
You came here to stay. Once more,
The pussy willows that come
After the New Year in this
Outlandish land are blooming.
There are deer and raccoon tracks
In the same places. A few
New sand bars and cobble beds
Have been left where erosion
Has gnawed deep into the hills.
The rounds of life are narrow.
War and peace have past like ghosts.
The human race sinks towards

Oblivion. A bittern
Calls from the same rushes where
You heard one on our first year
In the West; and where I heard
One again in the year
Of your death.

KINGS RIVER CANYON

My sorrow is so wide
I cannot see across it;
And so deep I shall never
Reach the bottom of it.
The moon sinks through deep haze,
As though the Kings River Canyon
Were filled with fine, warm, damp gauze.
Saturn gleams through the thick light
Like a gold, wet eye; nearby,
Antares glows faintly,
Without sparkle. Far overhead,
Stone shines darkly in the moonlight—
Lookout Point, where we lay
In another full moon, and first
Peered down into this canyon.
Here we camped, by still autumnal
Pools, all one warm October.
I baked you a bannock birthday cake.
Here you did your best paintings—
Innocent, wondering landscapes.
Very few of them are left
Anywhere. You destroyed them
In the terrible trouble
Of your long sickness. Eighteen years
Have passed since that autumn.
There was no trail here then.
Only a few people knew

How to enter this canyon.
We were all alone, twenty
Miles from anybody;
A young husband and wife,
Closed in and wrapped about
In the quiet autumn,
In the sound of quiet water,
In the turning and falling leaves,
In the wavering of innumerable
Bats from the caves, dipping
Over the odorous pools
Where the great trout drowsed in the evenings.

Eighteen years have been ground
To pieces in the wheels of life.
You are dead. With a thousand
Convicts they have blown a highway
Through Horseshoe Bend. Youth is gone,
That only came once. My hair
Is turning grey and my body
Heavier. I too move on to death.
I think of Henry King's stilted
But desolate *Exequy*,
Of Yuan Chen's great poem,
Unbearably pitiful;
Alone by the Spring river
More alone than I had ever
Imagined I would ever be,
I think of Frieda Lawrence,
Sitting alone in New Mexico,
In the long drought, listening
For the hiss of the milky Isar,
Over the cobbles, in a lost Spring.

LI CH'ING-CHAO (1084–1151)

On Plum Blossoms
TO THE TUNE "A LITTLE WILD GOOSE"

This morning I woke
In a bamboo bed with paper curtains.
I have no words for my weary sorrow,
No fine poetic thoughts.
The sandalwood incense smoke is stale,
The jade burner is cold.
I feel as though I were filled with quivering water.
To accompany my feelings
Someone plays three times on a flute
"Plum Blossoms Are Falling
in a Village by the River."
How bitter this Spring is.
Small wind, fine rain, *hsiao, hsiao,*
Falls like a thousand lines of tears.
The flute player is gone.
The jade tower is empty.
Broken hearted—we had relied on each other.
I pick a plum branch,
But my man has gone beyond the sky,
And there is no one to give it to.

Translated from the Chinese by Kenneth Rexroth and Ling Chung

HSU CHAO (ca. 1200)

The Locust Swarm

Locusts laid their eggs in the corpse
Of a soldier. When the worms were
Mature, they took wing. Their drone
Was ominous, their shells hard.
Anyone could tell they had hatched
From an unsatisfied anger.
They flew swiftly towards the North.
They hid the sky like a curtain.
When the wife of the soldier
Saw them, she turned pale, her breath
Failed her. She knew he was dead
In battle, his corpse lost in
The desert. That night she dreamed
She rode a white horse, so swift
It left no footprints, and came
To where he lay in the sand.
She looked at his face, eaten
By the locusts, and tears of
Blood filled her eyes. Ever after
She would not let her children
Injure any insect which
Might have fed on the dead. She
Would lift her face to the sky
And say, "O locusts, if you
Are seeking a place to winter,
You can find shelter in my heart."

Translated from the Chinese by Kenneth Rexroth

KAKINOMOTO NO HITOMARO (662–710)

from *Three Naga Uta*

When she was still alive
We would go out, arm in arm,
And look at the elm trees
Growing on the embankment
In front of our house.
Their branches were interlaced.
Their crowns were dense with spring leaves.
They were like our love.
Love and trust were not enough to turn back
The wheels of life and death.
She faded like a mirage over the desert.
One morning like a bird she was gone
in the white scarves of death.
Now when the child
Whom she left in her memory
Cries and begs for her,
All I can do is pick him up
And hug him clumsily.
I have nothing to give him.
In our bedroom our pillows
Still lie side by side,
As we lay once.
I sit there by myself
And let the days grow dark.
I lie awake at night, sighing till daylight.
No matter how much I mourn
I shall never see her again.
They tell me her spirit
May haunt Mount Hagai
Under the eagles' wings.
I struggle over the ridges
And climb to the summit.
I know all the time

That I shall never see her,
Not even so much as a faint quiver in the air.
All my longing, all my love
Will never make any difference.

Translated from the Japanese by Kenneth Rexroth

SAPPHO (ca. 630–570 B.C.)

Two Fragments

O Pollyanna
Polyanaktidas,
Good-bye, good-bye.

    *

[   ]
      toward
[
      should you be willing
      few
      to be borne
      any
      regard that pleasure
      you know and
      have forgotten but grief
[
      if any speak
      for I also
      no longer than to the day after tomorrow
      to be loved
      love, I say, will become strong
[
      and grievous
      sharp
[
      and know this
      whoever you
      will love
[
[
      of the arrows
[   ]

Translated from the Greek by Guy Davenport

LOUISE LABÉ (ca. 1520–1566)

Sonnet 23

Then what does it avail me, that you once
Sang so divinely of my golden hair?
And that you once, in passion, could declare
That my two eyes were like two separate suns

Whose fires the god had gathered from above
To strike you down? And what of all those hot,
Distracted tears and deathless vows? And what
Of death itself, which was to crown your love?

Was this your stratagem? That you appear
Enslaved while you enslave me? O, my dear,
Forgive me this suspicion! Dazed, drawn under

By all this grief, I know not what to do
Except once more console myself that you
Also will grieve, wherever you may wander.

Translated from the French by Frederic Prokosch

SUSAN HOWE (b. 1937)

FROM *THAT THIS*

from *The Disappearance Approach*
IN MEMORY OF PETER H. HARE (1935–2008)

Starting from nothing with nothing when everything else has been said

—

"O My Very Dear Child. What shall I say? A holy and good God has covered us with a dark cloud." On April 3, 1758, Sarah Edwards wrote this in a letter to her daughter Esther Edwards Burr when she heard of Jonathan's sudden death in Princeton. For Sarah all works of God are a kind of language or voice to instruct us in things pertaining to calling and confusion. I love to read her husband's analogies, metaphors, and similes.

For Jonathan and Sarah all rivers run into the sea yet the sea is not full, so in general there is always progress as in the revolution of a wheel and each soul comes upon the call of God in his word. I read words but don't hear God in them.

—

We can't be limited to just this anxious life.

—

Now—putting bits of memory together, trying to pick out the good while doing away with the bad—I'm left with one overwhelming impression—the unpresentable violence of a negative double.

—

He was lying with his head on his arm, the way I had often seen him lie asleep. I thought of Steerforth's drowned body in *David Copperfield*, also the brutality of sending young children away to boarding school in order to forge important ties for future life. Though Steerforth is a sadistic character his perfect name forms a second skin. Something has to remain to rest a soul against stone.

—

Land of darkness or darkness itself you shadow mouth.

—

Maybe there is some not yet understood return to people we have loved and lost. I need to imagine the possibility even if I don't believe it.

—

The paperwhites are blooming wonderfully. They resemble February in its thin clarity. Spare white blooms against watery green leaves and white and off-white pebbles around each ochre half-exposed bulb: the blue hyacinth I bought at Stop & Shop is also flowering. Alone with the tremendous silence of your absence, I want to fill this room between our workspaces with flowers because light flows through them—their scent is breath or spirit of life against my dread of being alone—of being cheated by people—today the electrician—next week Greco and Haynes for the well water filter.

—

Sorrows have been passed and unknown continents approached.

—

Outside the field of empirically possible knowledge is there a property of blueness in itself that continues to exist when everything else is sold away?

—

Returning home, after only a day or two away, I often have the sense of intruding on infinite and finite local evocations and wonder how things are, in relation to how they appear. This sixth sense of another reality even in simplest objects is what poets set out to show but cannot once and for all.

If there is an afterlife, then we still might: if not, not.

from *Frolic Architecture*

set at great distance from this world, ‹
it then appeared to me a vain, toilsom·
tants were strangely wandered, lost, &
:omfort to me that I was so separatec
rldly affairs, by my present affliction&
tho melancholy was yet in a quiet frame
iers I was in, it was not without a deep
irenared for Death, & I did set myself tr

YOEL HOFFMANN (b. 1937)

from *The Heart is Katmandu*

16

Suddenly, for no reason, his heart breaks.

His red heart which has seen all sorts of things—streets, candles burning in the night, countless feet—this heart gives way out of loneliness and fear.

There is no longer anything to hold on to (Yehoahim thinks) and he weeps like a jackal, or an owl, or a legendary river that sweeps along what it sweeps along, with neither purpose nor end.

93

Later on, when Elizabeth died, Ephraim went at one to the cemetery and the day was delightful. There was a big taxi and someone shouted "Charity saves from death."

The shirt, Ephraim, the Bank Café, and Batya (he thinks) are like the stuff of a great novel someone is writing and the only thing missing is someone (like the foreman he saw once) who will always be shouting "There's no time."

135

My wife left me, Yehoahim says.

He sees the empty house and Nitza-the-closet but now the pain has grown dull, as though it were coming from the other side of the wall.

Batya runs the fingers of her free hand over Yehoahim's chin, and makes the sound of a B-flat.

(Imagine, for a moment, the death of God. That great body ceases to breathe and nevertheless we're all within it.)

161

He raises a plate and says blue blue blue blue blue blue
blue blue blue blue blue blue blue blue blue blue blue
blue blue blue blue blue blue blue blue blue blue blue
blue blue blue blue blue blue blue blue blue blue blue

182

On the way back home from the clinic Batya sees the
trees' shadows which, in December, are naked as the trees
themselves, and her own shadow and the shadow of the
baby carriage pass through the treetops.

An inner voice tells her Cry, Cry, and therefore tears
stream down her cheeks, like what one sometimes sees
on the walls of apartments when the plaster begins to
crumble.

There is no end to it (she thinks), and nevertheless here
I am walking around under the sun.

Translated from the Hebrew by Peter Cole

OCTAVIO PAZ (1914–1998)

Interrupted Elegy

Today I remember the dead in my house.
We'll never forget the first death,
though he died in a flash, so suddenly
he never reached his bed or the holy oil.
I hear his cane hesitating on a step of the staircase,
the body gaining strength with a sigh,
the door that opens, the corpse that enters.
From a door to dying there's little space
and hardly enough time to sit down,
raise your head, look at the clock,
and realize: it's eight-fifteen.

Today I remember the dead in my house.
The woman who died night after night
and her dying was a long goodbye,
a train that never left.
The greed of her mouth,
hanging on the thread of a sigh,
her eyes never closing, making signs,
wandering from the lamp to my eyes,
a fixed gaze that embraces another gaze,
far off, that suffocates in the embrace
and in the end escapes and watches from the riverbank
how the soul sinks and loses its body
and finds no eyes to grab hold on…
Was that gaze inviting me to die?
Perhaps we die only because no one
wants to die with us, no one
wants to look us in the eye.

Today I remember the dead in my house.
The one who left for a few hours
and no one knew into what silence he had gone.
After dinner, each night,

the colorless pause that leads to emptiness
or the endless sentence half-hanging
from the spider's thread of silence
opens a corridor for him to return:
we hear his footsteps, he climbs, he stops…
And someone among us gets up
and closes the door shut.
But he, on the other side, insists.
He lies in wait in every recess and hollow,
he wanders among yawns, at the edge of things.
Though we shut the door, he insists.

Today I remember the dead in my house.
Faces forgotten in my mind, faces
without eyes, staring eyes, emptied out:
Am I searching in them for my secret,
the god of blood my blood moves,
the god of ice, the god who devours me?
His silence is the mirror of my life,
in my life his death is prolonged,
I am the final error of his errors.

Today I remember the dead in my house.
The scattered thoughts, the scattered
act, the names strewn
(lacunae, empty zones, holes
where stubborn memory rummages)
the dispersion of encounters,
the ego with its abstract wink, always shared
with another ego that is the same, the rages,
desire and its masks, the buried
snake, the slow erosions,
the hope, the fear, the act
and its opposite: within me they persist,
they beg to eat the bread, the fruit, the body,
to drink the water that was denied to them.

But there is no water now, everything is dry,
the bread is tasteless, the fruit bitter,
love domesticated, masticated,
in cages with invisible bars,
the onanist ape and the trained bitch,
what you devour devours you,
your victim is also your executioner.
Heap of dead days, crumpled newspapers,
and nights stripped of bark,
and in the dawn of the swollen eyelids,
the gesture with which we undo
the running knot, the necktie,
and now the lights have gone out in the streets
—*greet the sun, spider, be not rancorous*—
and more dead than living go off to bed.

The world is a circular desert,
heaven is closed and hell empty.

Translated from the Spanish by Eliot Weinberger

MURIEL RUKEYSER (1913–1980)

First Elegy: Rotten Lake

As I went down to Rotten Lake I remembered
the wrecked season, haunted by plans of salvage,
snow, the closed door, footsteps and resurrections,
      machinery of sorrow.

The warm grass gave to the feet and the stilltide water
was floor of evening and magnetic light and
reflection of wish, the black-haired beast with my eyes
      walking beside me.

The green and yellow lights, the street of water standing
point to the image of that house whose destruction
I weep when I weep you. My door (no), poems, rest,
      (don't say it!) untamable need.

*

When you have left the river you are a little way
nearer the lake; but I leave many times.
Parents parried my past; the present was poverty,
the future depended on my unfinished spirit.
There was no misgivings because there was no choice,
only regret for waste, and the wild knowledge:
growth and sorry and discovery.

When you have left the river you proceed alone;
all love is likely to be illicit; and few
friends to command the soul; they are too feeble.
Rejecting the subtle and contemplative minds
as being too thin in the bone; and the gross thighs
and unevocative hands fail also. But the poet
and his wife, those who say Survive, remain;
and those two who were with me on the ship
leading me to the sum of the years, in Spain.

When you have left the river you will hear the war.
In the mountains, with tourists, in the insanest groves
the sound of kill, the precious face of peace.
And the sad frightened child, continual minor,
returns, nearer whole circle, O and nearer
all that was loved, the lake, the naked river,
what must be crossed and cut out of your heart,
what must be stood beside and straightly seen.

*

As I went down to Rotten Lake I remembered
how the one crime is need. The man lifting the loaf
with hunger as motive can offer no alibi, is
           always condemned.

These are the lines at the employment bureau
and the tense students at their examinations;
needing makes clumsy and robs them of their wish,
           in one fast gesture

plants on them failure of the imagination;
and lovers who lower their bodies into the chair
gently and sternly as if the flesh had been wounded,
           never can conquer.

Their need is too great, their vulnerable bodies
rigidly joined will snap, turn love away,
fear parts them, they lose their hands and voices, never
           get used to the world.

Walking at night, they are asked Are you your best friend's
best friend? and must say No, not yet, they are
love's vulnerable, and they go down to Rotten Lake
     hoping for wonders.

Dare it arrive, the day when weakness ends?
When the insistence is strong, the wish converted?
I prophesy the meeting by the water
        of these desires.

I know what this is, I have known the waking
when every night ended in one cliff-dream
of faces drowned beneath the porous rock
        brushed by the sea;

suffered the change: deprived erotic dreams
of images of that small house where peace
walked room to room and always with one face
        telling her stories,

and needed that, past loss, past fever, and the
attractive enemy who in my bed
touches all night the body of my sleep,
        improves my summer

with madness, impossible loss, and the dead music
of altered promise, a room torn up by the roots,
the desert that crosses from the door to the wall,
        continual bleeding,

and all the time that will which cancels enmity,
seeks its own Easter, arrives at the water-barrier;
must face it now, biting the lakeside ground;
        looks for its double,

the twin that must be met again, changeling need,
blazing in color somewhere, flying yellow
into the forest with its lucid edict:
        take to the world,

this is the honor of your flesh, the offering
of strangers, the faces of cities, honor of all your wish.
Immortal undoing! I say in my own voice. These prophecies
        may all come true,

out of the beaten season. I look in Rotten Lake,
wait for the flame reflection, seeing only
the free beast flickering black along my side
        animal of my need,

and cry I want! I want! rising among the world
to gain my converted wish, the amazing desire
that keeps me alive, though the face be still, be still,
the slow dilated heart know nothing but lack,
now I begin again the private rising,
the ride to survival of that consuming bird
beating, up from dead lakes, ascents of fire.

THOMAS HARDY (1840–1928)

"I found her out there"

I found her out there
On a slope few see,
That falls westwardly
To the salt-edged air,
Where the ocean breaks
On the purple strand,
And the hurricane shakes
The solid land.

I brought her here,
And have laid her to rest
In a noiseless nest
No sea beats near.
She will never be stirred
In her loamy cell
By the waves long heard
And loved so well.

So she does not sleep
By those haunted heights
The Atlantic smites
And the blind gales sweep,
Whence she often would gaze
At Dundagel's famed head,
While the dipping blaze
Dyed her face fire-red;

And would sigh at the tale
Of sunk Lyonnesse,
As a wind-tugged tress
Flapped her cheek like a flail;
Or listen at whiles
With a thought-bound brow
To the murmuring miles
She is far from now.

Yet her shade, maybe,
Will creep underground
Till it catch the sound
Of that western sea
As it swells and sobs
Where she once domiciled,
And joy in its throbs
With the heart of a child.

EUGÉNIO DE ANDRADE (1923–2005)

Brief September Elegy

I don't know how you came,
but there must be a road
leading back from death.

You are seated in the garden,
your hands in your lap, filled with sweetness,
your eyes resting on the last roses
of these vast and calm September days.

What music do you follow so intently
that you don't even notice me?
What forest, or river, or sea?
Or is it within yourself
that everything still sings?

I would like to speak to you,
just to tell you that I'm here,
but I'm afraid,
afraid the music all will stop
and you will cease to see the roses.
Afraid of breaking the thread
with which you weave unremembered days.

With what words
or kisses or tears
can one awake the dead without harming them,
without bringing them to that black foam
where bodies and bodies repeat themselves,
parsimoniously, among shadows?

Stay as you are then,
filled with sweetness,
seated, gazing at the roses,
and so very far away
you don't even notice me.

Translated from the Portuguese by Alexis Levitin

MEI-MEI BERSSENBRUGGE (b. 1947)

Slow Down, Now

1

I've been sitting looking at a plant, without feeling time at all, and my breathing is calm.

There are tiny white rosettes, and the whole bush is a glory of feathery pink seedheads, here in the arroyo.

Even with closed eyes I see roses in the center of my sight, new ones opening with pink petals illuminated by the low sun behind me, and gray green leaves.

There's no stopping this effusion.

Looking at the plant releases my boundaries, so time is not needed for experience.

Late afternoon is like a stage, a section of vaster landscape, and my mood is of a summer idyll.

The dry arroyo sparkles all around.

Meaning I come upon on wild land strikes me at first as a general impression, then joy suffuses me.

I accept that I've aged and some friends have died.

At first, meaning is part of the rose, not unified with my experience as a whole, the way my sight opens out to its peripheries.

There's an impasse between my will, desire and the resistance of a phenomenon to reveal itself.

My seeing becomes so slow, it seems to disengage; it grows cloudy; then suddenly, meaning as a whole interweaves with my perception.

A delicate empiricism makes itself identical with my plant.

2

I repeat the words freshness, tenderness, softness, the happiness of birds, as if speaking directly to a plant.

Sun lights the profusion of pink plumes, thousands of feathery seeds already reaching into empty space where I've taken a branch.

That space was left open by the vision I'm having now!

I hold my first sight of the Apache plume and this moment next to each other; I go back and forth, comparing them.

I see her multiple aspects as living representations, her symbiosis with birds, relation to original plants, fragrance, one as medicine of the oracle.

These aspects are not referred to, not associative, but intrinsic to my sight, as slowly gaps diminish and missing images appear or experience fills in; one transforms to another along an extending multidimensional axis of seeing a plant.

It's not a metaphor for the flow of our surroundings.

3

One day you need a plant you don't know, in order to connect pieces in yourself, or in a person you're trying to be with.

It may be a rosebush at the end of the road, a summer rose, whitish on the outside of each petal and pink inside, expressing its gestalt visually.

When a plant receives this kind of communication, it begins altering chemicals its wavelengths reflect, in order to offer itself to your imaginal sight, for you to gather it.

The plant or another person awakes from embedding in the livingness of the world and takes notice of your request.

The internal chemistry of plants is one primary language of response that they possess.

Through this method of your perception of its color, its fragrance, an infusion of its petals, you not only receive molecules of plant compound itself, but also meaning in yourself the plant is responding to, so there is meaning in a chemical compound.

4
Even though the rose I want is in the garden of my friend I miss, another reveals itself in late light in the arroyo when I'm alone, a wild rose, Delphic.

Illness is not healed simply by supplying something rose-colored and lovely as a medicinal opiate.

The beauty provides form for meaning, and though it does help my body, form to form, I'm not only what my senses perceive, and my disease not just a physical absence virus fills.

When my fluctuating electromagnetic field touches that of another person, plant or entity, emotion is my perception of data encoded in that field.

So, when a plant projects coherent energy, others respond and become more animated, open, connected.

They use this amplified field to shift biological function.

DNA alters; there's communication across distance.

Organisms can intentionally insert information to strengthen cooperative interactions among, for example, an Apache plume, ants and an agave in the riverbed, like human families whose interweaving, loving bonds represent the long term incorporation of supportive, co-evolutionary fields continually embedding complex new data.

You and I nest within many such fields from a rose.

HANS FAVEREY (1930–1990)

Three Poems from *Sequence Against Death*

*

The eyes which grant
my eyes her eyes,
because this is how

the light in them goes between;

the bracken, once I, stepping out of the stream,
was walking up the slope and smelt the woods;
the sweet chestnuts in the basket,
in the print on the wall
by the balcony;

the stylish new shoes you will be
taking on your journey tomorrow.

*

Is the same not good enough then;
or does it hurt more really than then.

But what then is love;

and is it right to love,
and grip to the mortal.
And so to grip the helm;
to row upriver, against
the current, even if it doesn't

get me half a boat-length forward;
if the stubborn willows cannot help
doing what has to come to pass, in
the name and honor of their seasons.

*

Its only riddle: *how*
it is; how that leaves it

at a loss, at less
than a loss, for words.

That I'm standing straight among rising plants.
That what encircles me like a world
takes possession of me, just as
what I keep veiled like a mist
wants to be possessed

by me. Listen! as the stone
splits the stream, so the chestnut keeps
its shiny silence; the antlion will never
embrace its ant and help it out of the funnel,
back to its antlike freedom.

Translated from the Dutch by Francis R. Jones

MICHAEL PALMER (b. 1943)

THREE POEMS FROM *THREAD*

Fragment After Dante

And I saw myself in the afterlife of rivers and fields
among the wandering souls and light-flecked paths.

There I was amazed to find
the damned and the innocent

commingled so, torturers and victims,
masters, sycophants and slaves

idling arm in arm, chatting
about nothing, about the fullness and ripeness

of nothing, the pleasures of the day
and of the hearth fires to follow

in the evening calm.
And they turned to me as one

and I heard their words, their
calls, each syllable, each phrase

but could not make them out.
And I saw myself struggling to wake,

howling and foaming like a dog,
biting at empty air.

Second Fragment

And she clasped my arm and said,
You, my son, who have lingered

too long among the dead, go
and return to the lighted shore

for those brief moments you have left
there among the hypocrites,

the torturers and deceivers
who've locked our republic in their thrall

as I'm told, for that far
I cannot see from this clouded place.

Then before my eyes her face
transformed from old to young,

that one I'd known in earliest youth,
and disappeared from view.

Thought (Third Fragment)

It is no light or simple thing
as Dante reminds us

in Canto 32
to render the absolute

bottom of the universe
amidst the piercing wails

of those self-devouring shades
locked in a lake of ice

their twisted, puss-
filled mouths

spewing endless shattered words
up towards this shattered earth

JOSÉ EMILIO PACHECO (b. 1939)

from *The Resting Place of Fire*

I:1
Nothing alters the disaster: the wealth
of hot blood transfuses the air with its grief.
At the sheer edge, what imminence or frontier
of rising wind already awaits us in the dawn?

With a coarse gasp
                    the air descends, in an
overweening gush comes inconsolably
down, even to the stoniest place for fire
                                        to take.

And sadly, like a leaf into the air, the blaze
struck up contemplates the incendiary thirst
of time, its eve of ruin, as if leaning out
over the sea, the steep stacks of the cities
wavering pale. What a blue peninsula
wobbling through pitch blackness the flame is,
there, plunged into the night.
So pale and haughty nevertheless;
hard-set, yet still serene, as if
                                struck dead.

II:5
Worlds veer back to tear apart. A star
Shoots raging by to war, until miraculously
it is shut, shipwrecked in the grass,
all its flying stuff blown out,
as if (like the tail of a bird) a falcon bolt
had snapped the vapor trailing from the star:
so it felt to the buried body
mangled in the embrace of mortal ground.

In Memoriam Luis Cernuda, November 5, 1963

6

While an acid uncertainty
cuts within the confines of the air,
I touch your memory—the urn
aroused.
And it is November, burnt leaf
of a tree that is no longer there
it lingers on,
sickening old scent
of this crowded heartache I have grown to be.

7

Every moment that goes, something wilts or grows.
Something has designs to endure, something remote
shapes the solid name for your suffering
into the sands (because the permanence
of their swell is there
where sea has ended in desert).

12

But is the world a gift from fire
or its own matter, weary
of never-ending
that brought itself into being?

III:2

All night I watched the fire grow.

3

In these past years the city has changed so
it isn't mine, anymore—the footfalls
echoed away into its vaults
never to step home.

Echoes footsteps memories all wreckage

Footsteps that are no longer there, your presence,
empty memory echoing in vain.
In a place that is no longer here, where you passed,
where I saw you last in the night,
this yesterday that waits for me in the tomorrow,
this future that crept back into history,
this continual today where I am losing you.

14 (*The sayings of Buddha*)
The whole world is in flames:
what is visible
                burns
and the burning eye investigates.
The fires of hate rage up.
The burning
usury and hurt.
Sorrow is a flame.
And anguish a great fire
in which all things
                burn.
In the cry of the flame
                the flames blaze up,
the world and the fire.
                So sad
and sorrowful, look at
                the falling leaf
blaze in the wind.

15
The poem is a fire
                and it does not last
A leaf in the wind
                too

too sad to say

Motionless now
                A bare space
until fire
rekindles inside
Each poem
                an epitaph for fire
a prisonhouse
                a flame
until in flames the silence settles
Sad   sad
                leaf in the wind
                                this blaze.

Translated from the Spanish by George McWhirter

ALLEN GROSSMAN (b. 1932)

Lament Fragment

Go down

(Forsaking the lagoons of bridged Atlantis)

To the mid-Atlantic ridge

                           where are the crazed
Magnetic fields and roped sheets, and stains
(The disordered fabric of the volcanic
Bed chamber) and the gigantic vermicular
Testimonies

             and stare upon the great
Principle of the solid world—the original
Torment trace.

               Go down, for down is the way,
And grapple one stone syllable
Of all that frozen love's discourse
Onto an iron dredge

             and on it rise
(Borne on the enormous weight of its desire
For light and the air)

             until it explodes
Upon the deck amid the astonished crew.

Then empty out the nets disposed about
Your person, and fill them with the pieces
Of that one vast syllable

                    and carry them
To Cahokia in East Saint Louis, where
My father was born who is dying now
(He was an honest man—mute as stone)

Place them on the top of Monk's Mound

(Go you. I am his son. I have no words.)

                                    and let

Them off like a siren.

BERNADETTE MAYER (b. 1945)

Sunday April 13

a clear cold sunny day, beautiful to some,
horrible to others. we're making maple
syrup again, smoke is rising from the evaporator,
it's hearty, everytime i begin to do something
something else intervenes, i wouldn't even think this
if i weren't in the mood to have the thought.
bernadette mayer, in a rush to put down her
weird thoughts, like everybody tells her to,
writes down too much, only a fraction of which is
even ever read because she is so disorganized,
plus she has had a brain hemorrhage, rendering her
even more mixed up in her constant thinking,
and she has lost the fine motor coordination
in her right hand—she can't handwrite. she has
to cook the chicken liver while phil is not in
the kitchen. at the moment her left knee is
so fucked she can barely walk, making the long
bushwhacking walks in the countryside that were able
to salvage her sanity, impossible. she tries
to do what others suggest but now she just plods on.
it's the last straw, hobbling from room to room,
hoping for change. she is lost but has no choice
she can't attempt suicide again for fear of failing.
she will cook the liver. She also cooks two pierogi,
eats them & sits in the sun

NATHANIEL TARN (b. 1928)

Sadness, They Say My Home

Sadness, they say my home, sadness,
what is the sadness say my life my living,
a diagram of death inside transparent flesh,
bonework jutting out right and left from spine,
building that prison-house from which no one emerges;
sadness, pool swum in one whole life, without an exit,
without a single daydream's exit any time,
moment, of day, of night, sadness: the motionless,
the inescapable, the color drained of color, tint drained
of tint, brightness of brightness, drained of all light;
sadness, the breath of flowers, the breath of birds,
the breath of simple things weaning from desolation,
the working permit of a dried up bone, the ghost
of all things tainted and disturbed. Now tired, now
desperately weary, the broken step and stagger,
the failure of the day, of every single day, of every
effort climbed along the ridges of a giant mountain,
climbed once again and one more once again and n;
sadness, the burden of our nights, blind nights and sleepless,
more sleepless than you there could ever think of being
sleepless, bone stuck into your ribs, holding you up,
something you think might be the spine;
sadness, I do not know, I do not carry knowledge,
I have no pocket for the secret prayers, I cannot think,
I cannot think philosophy, I cannot tell you life, or tell you
death, sadness because, sadness-preoccupation,
sadness the ancient used to call the "melancholia,"
blackness, the dying of the trees over the massive landscape
that caused this sorrow now, broke out an artery, opened
the veins onto the ground, letting blood flower—
but colorless, neutral and gray at times, anemic after sex,
rampant like lust at others, hot blood spurting out crimson;
sadness you see my house, never to heal, everyday house,
ever night house, never to be departed from, never again

to be beginning but always end, sadness an ending
of all things, the breaking of all things, the life I cannot leave—
the dark sun of this weeping, molten moon,
what is that star of sadness in the sky, behind the sun,
that cannot ever set, and cannot ever break, and cannot
ever drown into the sky: please allow dying now,
that dark abandonment among the sucked-out trees,
please allow coming home to sadness never drowning.

ZEAMI MOTOKIYO (1363–1443)

from Kinuta

WIFE: Sorrow!—
Sorrow is in the twigs of the duck's nest
And in the pillow of the fishes,
At being held apart in the waves,
Sorrow between mandarin ducks,
Who have been in love
Since time out of mind.
Sorrow—
There is more sorrow between the united
Though they move in the one same world.
O low 'Remembering-grass,'
I do not forget to weep
At the sound of the rain upon you,
My tears are a rain in the silence,
O heart of the seldom cleaning.

[. . .]

CHORUS: The time of regret comes not before the deed,
This we have heard from the eight thousand shadows.
This is their chorus—the shadowy blades of grass.
Sorrow! to be exchanging words
At the string-tip—
Sorrow! that we can but speak
With the bow-tip of the adzusa!
The way that a ghost returns
From the shadow of the grass—
We have heard the stories,
It is eight thousand times, they say,
Before regret runs in a smooth-worn groove,
Forestalls itself.

Translated from the Japanese by Ezra Pound and Ernest Fenellosa

KAMAU BRATHWAITE (b. 1930)

Blues

Wake up this mornin
sunshine int showin thru my door
wake up this mornin
sunshine int showin thru my door
cause the blues is got me
an i int got no strength to go no more

wake up this mornin
clothes still scatter cross the floor
wake up this morning
clothes still scatter cross the floor
loss night the ride was lovely
but she int comin back far more

sea island sunshine
whe are yu hidin now
sea island sunshine
whe are yu hidin now
cd a sware a leff yu in the cupboard
but is only empties mockin at me in
there now

empty bottles knockin
laugh like a woman satisfye
empty bottles knockin
laugh like a woman satisfye
she full & leff me empty
laughin when I shd a crie

this place is empty bottles
this place is a woman satisfrye
this place is empty bottles

this place is a woman satisfrye
she drink muh sugar water
til mah sunshine die

RIHAKU (701–762)

Lament of the Frontier Guard

By the North Gate, the wind blows full of sand,
  Lonely from the beginning of time until now!
  Trees fall, the grass goes yellow with autumn.
  I climb the towers and towers
      to watch out the barbarous land:
  Desolate castle, the sky, the wide desert.
  There is no wall left to this village
  Bones white with a thousand frosts,
  High heaps, covered with trees and grass;
  Who brought this to pass?
  Who has brought the army with drums and with kettle-drums?
  Barbarous kings.
  A gracious spring, turned to blood-ravenous autumn,
  A turmoil of wars-men, spread over the middle kingdom,
  Three hundred and sixty thousand,
  And sorrow, sorrow like rain.
  Sorrow to go, and sorrow, sorrow returning.
  Desolate, desolate fields,
  And no children of warfare upon them,
          No longer the men for offence and defence.
  Ah, how shall you know the dreary sorrow at the
          North Gate,
  With Rihaku's name forgotten,
  And we guardsmen fed to the tigers.

Translated from the Chinese by Ezra Pound

WILFRED OWEN (1893–1918)

Strange Meeting

It seemed that out of battle I escaped
Down some profound dull tunnel, long since scooped
Through granites which titanic wars had groined.
Yet also there encumbered sleepers groaned,
Too fast in thought or death to be bestirred.
Then, as I probed them, one sprang up, and stared
With piteous recognition in fixed eyes,
Lifting distressful hands as if to bless.
And by his smile, I knew that sullen hall,
By his dead smile I knew we stood in Hell.
With a thousand pains that vision's face was grained;
Yet no blood reached there from the upper ground,
And no guns thumped, or down the flues made moan.
"Strange friend," I said, "here is no cause to mourn."
"None," said that other, "save the undone years,
The hopelessness. Whatever hope is yours,
Was my life also; I went hunting wild
After the wildest beauty in the world,
Which lies not calm in eyes, or braided hair,
But mocks the steady running of the hour,
And if it grieves, grieves richlier than here.
For of my glee might many men have laughed,
And of my weeping something had been left,
Which must die now. I mean the truth untold,
The pity of war, the pity war distilled.
Now men will go content with what we spoiled,
Or, discontent, boil bloody, and be spilled.
They will be swift with swiftness of the tigress.
None will break ranks, though nations trek from progress.
Courage was mine, and I had mystery,
Wisdom was mine, and I had mastery:
To miss the march of this retreating world
Into vain citadels that are not walled.
Then, when much blood had clogged their chariot-wheels,

I would go up and wash them from sweet wells,
Even with truths that lie too deep for taint.
I would have poured my spirit without stint
But not through wounds; not on the cess of war.
Foreheads of men have bled where no wounds were.
I am the enemy you killed, my friend.
I knew you in this dark: for so you frowned
Yesterday through me as you jabbed and killed.
I parried; but my hands were loath and cold.
Let us sleep now...."

DUNYA MIKHAIL (b. 1965)

from *Diary of a Wave Outside the Sea*

Death always longs for us.
It comes from beyond the continents.
It crosses great distances with a basket of fire in its hands.
It gives us balls of fire to play with
until we forget the meaning of the sun!

The child kept looking for a pale moon
he had seen one day through the window.
Maybe it tumbled down in its sleep (what is sleep?)
Maybe the worms ate it (what are worms?)
Maybe it disappeared with the electricity (what is electricity?)
Maybe the storm has abated.
Maybe the storm hasn't yet begun.

They said: Fill the boxes with air
(inhale and exhale and nothing).

For what and for whom are we storing the air?
Fruit does not bear our crown
and shadows do not reflect our existence.

Noise fills the place,
as if a box was opened unexpectedly,
and piles of people,
cars, and suitcases fell out
into what, we don't know
and they don't know.

What kind of enchantment transformed the city,
shouting with life and commotion,
into a sleepy princess who waits for the prince's kiss
in order to yawn again?

What kind of hands sprinkle death over the trees
so that grains of wheat fall from shivering
beaks and the bulging eyes of birds
stiffen with broken eggs?

Since they are skyless eyes, they don't see the stars
shining over a falling bridge.

The gods have turned us into idols,
but they forgot to kill our feelings
so our sufferings continue into eternity.

We don't have remains.
We…
We are the remains.

Where are you rushing to with your ax?

The wars multiply
and discard us.
As for the other one,
he sets off on tiptoe over the graves,
on his way to another war.

Translated from the Arabic by Elizabeth Winslow

NATHANIEL MACKEY (b. 1947)

from *Day after Day of the Dead*
—*"mu" forty-eighth part*—

"While we're alive," we kept
repeating. Tongues, throats,
roofs of our mouths bone dry,
skeletons we'd someday
be...
Panicky masks we wore for
effect more than effect,
more real than we'd admit...

No longer wanting to know
what soul was, happy to
see
shadow, know touch...
Happy to have sun at our
backs, way led by shadow,
happy to have bodies, block
light...
Afternoon sun lighting leaf,
glint of glass, no matter what,
about to be out of body it
seemed...
Soon to be shadowless we thought,
said we thought, not to be offguard,
caught out. Gray morning we
meant
to be done with, requiem so
sweet we forgot what it lamented,
teeth
turning to sugar, we
grinned

•

Day after day of the dead we were
   desperate. Dark what the night
before we saw lit, bones we'd
      eventually be... At day's end a
                              new
   tally but there it was, barely
                              begun,
   rock the clock tower let go of,
      iridescent headstone, moment's
   rebuff... Soul, we saw, said we
                              saw,
invisible imprint. No one wanted to
                              know
   what soul was... Day after day of
      the dead we were deaf, numb to
   what the night before we said moved
                              us,
   fey light's coded locale... I fell away,
we momentarily gone, deaf but to
      brass's obsequy, low brass's
   croon begun. I fell away, not fast,
                              floated,
      momentary mention an accord
   with the wind, day after day of the dead
   the same as day before day of

the dead... "No surprise," I fell away
   muttering, knew no one would
                              hear,
   not even
   me

TU FU (712–770)

Parting in Old Age

Vanished in all four directions—peace,
peace old age will never bring. My
sons and grandsons all war-dead,
why live this body's life out alone?

Tossing my cane aside, I set out, pitiful
sight even to fellow soldiers—a man
lucky to have these few teeth left
now the marrow is dried from his bones.

Among armor-clad warriors, I offer
deep farewell bows to the magistrate,
and my dear wife lies by the roadside
sobbing, her winter clothes worn paper-

thin. This death's farewell wounds me
again with her bitter cold. From this,
no return. And still, she calls out
behind me: *You must eat more—please.*

T'u-men's wall is strong, Hsing-yüan
ferry formidable. It's not like Yeh.
Though no less certain, death won't come
suddenly. Life is separation and return,

is plentiful one day, and the next
withered. It is the nature of things, I
know, but thinking of our shared youth,
I look back slowly, heart-stricken.

Nothing in ten thousand kingdoms but war.
Beacon-fires smother ridges and peaks.
Grasslands and forests reeking of the dead,
Blood turns brooks and springs cinnabar-red.

Not an untormented village left anywhere,
how can I hesitate, how avoid this life
torn loose from my calm, thatched-home
life laying my insides out bare to ruin.

Translated from the Chinese by David Hinton

BEI DAO (b. 1949)

Requiem
FOR THE VICTIMS OF JUNE FOURTH

Not the living but the dead
under the doomsday-purple sky
go in groups
suffering guides forward suffering
at the end of hatred is hatred
the spring has run dry, the conflagration stretches unbroken
the road back is even further away

Not gods but the children
amid the clashing of helmets
say their prayers
mothers breed light
darkness breeds mothers
the stone rolls, the clock runs backward
the eclipse of the sun has already taken place

Not your bodies but your souls
shall share a common birthday every year
you are all the same age
love has founded for the dead
an everlasting alliance
you embrace each other closely
in the massive register of deaths

*Translated from the Chinese
by Bonnie S. McDougall and Chen Maiping*

RUDAKI (858–954)

Young or Old We Die

Young or old we die
for every neck a noose
though the rope be long for some,

struggle or calm
broke or a king
life's but wind
        and a dream
perhaps describing
some other thing;
and with the end
all will be the same again
and all will be well.

Translated from the Persian by Omar Pound

CHRISTINA ROSSETTI (1830–1894)

A Better Resurrection

I have no wit, no words, no tears;
  My heart within me like a stone
Is numbed too much for hopes or fears;
  Look right, look left, I dwell alone;
I lift mine eyes, but dimmed with grief
  No everlasting hills I see;
My life is in the falling leaf:
  O Jesus, quicken me.

My life is like a faded leaf,
  My harvest dwindled to a husk;
Truly my life is void and brief
  And tedious in the barren dusk;
My life is like a frozen thing,
  No bud nor greenness can I see:
Yet rise it shall – the sap of Spring;
  O Jesus, rise in me.

My life is like a broken bowl,
  A broken bowl that cannot hold
One drop of water for my soul
  Or cordial in the searching cold;
Cast in the fire the perished thing,
  Melt and remould it, till it be
A royal cup for Him my King:
  O Jesus, drink of me.

ROSMARIE WALDROP (b. 1935)

Of Death and Burial

He that hath death in his house blackes his face. Soot clotted with tears and gaping with vowels. **They abhorre to mention the dead by the name** sealed into their lips, the bleeding stump of their tongues. **Sachimaûpan. He That Was Prince Here** is wrapped in wailing, in flexion, in hands before the face, in smaller and smaller particles. Perspective unsettled by chemical methods. They bury sideways **the mat he died on, the dish he ate from**, the empty regions of his body, and sometimes hang his shadow upon the next tree which none will touch but suffer to rot.

    occlude
    occult
    orthodox
    haphazard
    obsolete
    irreparable

Solitude in heat. I resented my lover turning his back on me for other mournful realities. Though each crossing of space casually implicates the flesh, attraction increasing faster than distance diminishes, I found myself alone among the rubble of love. I had finally reached the center of the city. It was deserted, in ruins, as useless as my birth and as permanent a site of murder.

    a hitch in time
    then the world changed
    then there was no memory
    then life could not
    be understood forward
    or backward

QU YUAN (ca. 340–278 B.C.)

from *Tian Wen: A Chinese Book of Origins*

What virtue moves the moon
To flourish after death?

*

Life is long here, and there is no death,
What is the end of longevity?

*

Heaven's mandate is not assured.
Who is punished, who succored?

*

Cast out on the ice,
How was he sheltered by the birds?

*

He hung by the neck from a tree.
Why did he take his life?

*

Lost at dusk in a thunderstorm,
What sorrow awaited the king's return?

Translated from the Chinese by Stephen Field

XI CHUAN (b. 1963)

Twilight

in the vast expanse of a nation
twilight is equally vast
lamp after lamp lights up
and twilight spreads out like autumn

oh deceased, appear now
all of the living have shut their mouths
where are you, deceased?
the twilight invites you to speak

some names I will memorize
some names search for their tombstones
countless names I've written down
as if I were writing a nation

and twilight spreads over the earth
an outstretched hand grasped
as twilight reaches the window, where someone
is always rapping lightly at my door

Translated from the Chinese by Lucas Klein

DANTE ALIGHIERI (1265–1321)

Sonnet

ON THE 9TH OF JUNE 1290

Upon a day, came Sorrow in to me,
    Saying, "I've come to stay with thee a while";
    And I perceived that she had ushered Bile
And Pain into my house for company.
Wherefore I said, "Go forth—away with thee!"
    But like a Greek she answered, full of guile,
    And went on arguing in an easy style,
Then, looking, I saw Love come silently,
Habited in black raiment, smooth and new,
    Having a black hat set upon his hair;
And certainly the tears he shed were true.
    So that I asked, "What ails thee, trifler?"
Answering he said: "A grief to be gone through;
    For our own lady's dying, brother dear."

Translated from the Italian by Dante Gabriel Rossetti

ROBERT DUNCAN (1919–1988)

After A Long Illness

No faculty not   ill at ease
        lets us
        begin where I must

from the failure of systems   breath
        less,   heart
        and lungs water-logd.

Clogged with light chains   the kidneys'
        condition is terminal   life

the light and the heavy,   the light
        and dark.   It has always been
close upon a particular Death, un
        disclosed   what's behind

seeing, feeling, tasting, smelling   —that Cloud!

For two years
bitterness pervaded:

in the physical body   the high   blood pressure
        the accumulation of toxins, the
break-down of ratios,

in the psyche   "stewd in its own juices"
        the eruption of hatreds,   the prayer
—I didn't have a prayer—   your care
        alone kept my love clear.

I will be there again   the ways
        must become crosst   and again
        dark passages,   dangerous straits.

My Death attended me and I knew
     I was not going to die,
nursed me thru.   Life took hold.

     What I ate   I threw up
and crawled thru as if turnd inside out.
     Every thought I had I saw
sickened me.   Secretly
     in the dark   the filters
     of my kidneys   petrified   and my Death
rearranged the date He has with me.

*

Yes, I was afraid
of not seeing you again,   of being
     taken away, not
of dying, the specter I have long
     known as my Death is the
Lord of a Passage that unites us;
     but of
     never having come to you that other
specter of my actually living is.
     Adamant.

"I have given you a cat in the dark," the voice said.
Everything changed in what has always been there
at work in the Ground: the two titles
     "Before the War", and now, "In the Dark"
underwrite the grand design.   The magic
     has always been there,   the magnetic purr
     run over me, the feel as of cat's fur
charging the refusal to feel.   That black stone
     now I see, has its electric familiar.

In the real I have always known myself
     in this realm where no Wind   stirs
     no Night
turns in turn to Day,   the Pool of the motionless water,
     the absolute Stillness.   In the World, death after death.
In this realm,   no last thrall of Life stirs.
     The imagination alone knows this condition.
As if this were before the War, before
     What Is,   in the dark this state
that knows nor sleep nor waking, nor dream
      —an eternal arrest.

GEORGE OPPEN (1908–1984)

Till Other Voices Wake Us

the generations

and the solace

of flight memory

of adolescence with my father
in France we stared
at monuments as tho we treaded

water stony

waters of the monuments and so turned
then hurriedly

on our course
before we might grow tired
and so drown and writing

thru the night (a young man,
Brooklyn, 1929) I named the book

series empirical
series all force
in events the myriad

lights have entered
us it is music more powerful

than music

till other voices wake
us or we drown

GEORGE HERBERT (1593–1633)

The Flower

How fresh, O Lord, how sweet and clean
Are thy returns! ev'n as the flowers in spring;
     To which, besides their own demean,
The late-past frosts tributes of pleasure bring.
                    Grief melts away
                    Like snow in May,
          As if there were no such cold thing.

     Who would have thought my shrivel'd heart
Could have recover'd greennesse? It was gone
     Quite under ground; as flowers depart
To see their mother-root, when they have blown;
                    Where they together
                    All the hard weather,
          Dead to the world, keep house unknown.

     These are thy wonders, Lord of power,
Killing and quickning, bringing down to hell
     And up to heaven in an houre:
Making a chiming of a passing-bell.
                    We say amisse,
                    This or that is:
          Thy word is all, if we could spell.

     O that I once past changing were,
Fast in thy Paradise, where no flower can wither!
     Many a spring I shoot up fair,
Offering at heav'n, growing and groning thither;
                    Nor doth my flower
                    Want a spring-showre,
          My sinnes and I joining together:

But while I grow in a straight line,
Still upwards bent, as if heav'n were mine own,
    Thy anger comes, and I decline:
What frost to that? what pole is not the zone,
            Where all things burn,
            When thou dost turn,
    And the least frown of thine is shown?

    And now in age I bud again,
After so many deaths I live and write;
    I once more smell the dew and rain,
And relish versing: O my onely Light,
            It cannot be
            That I am he
    On whom thy tempests fell all night.

    These are thy wonders, Lord of love,
To make us see we are but flowers that glide:
    Which when we once can finde and prove,
Thou hast a garden for us, where to bide.
            Who would be more,
            Swelling through store,
    Forfeit their Paradise by their pride.

C. H. SISSON (1914–2003)

April

Exactly: where the winter was
The spring has come: I see her now
In the fields, and as she goes
The flowers spring, nobody knows how.

PHILIPPE JACCOTTET (b. 1925)

from *Seedtime*

Let silent grief at least
Hatch out that last chance
Of light.

Let that extremity of wretchedness
Preserve the chance of flowers.

Translated from the French by Michael Hamburger

GUILLAME APOLLINAIRE (1880–1918)

The Farewell

I picked this fragile sprig of heather
Autumn has died long since remember
Never again shall we see one another
Odor of time sprig of heather
Remember I await our time together

Translated from the French by Roger Shattuck

H.D. (1886–1961)

from *The Walls Do Not Fall*

Grant us strength to endure
a little longer,

now the heart's alabaster
is broken;

we would feed forever
on the amber honey-comb

of your remembered greeting,
but the old-self,

still half at-home in the world,
cries out in anger,

I am hungry, the children cry for food
and flaming stones fall on them;

our awareness leaves us defenseless;
O, for your Presence

among the fishing-nets
by the beached boats on the lake-edge;

when, in the drift of wood-smoke,
will you say again, as you said,

the baked fish is ready,
here is the bread?

Epitaph

So I may say,
"I died of living,
having lived one hour";

so they may say,
"she died soliciting
illicit fervour";

so you may say,
"Greek flower; Greek ecstasy
reclaims for ever

one who died
following
intricate songs' lost measure."

CHUANG-TZU (ca. 369–286 B.C.)

from *The Wisdom of the Taoists*

The wife of Chuang-tzu died and his friend Hui-tzu went to condole with him. Chuang-tzu was sitting with his legs spread out, pounding on a tub and singing. Hui-tzu said: Here is someone who has lived with you, brought up your children, and grown old. Not to weep at her death is surely bad enough, but to beat on a tub and sing, surely that is going too far. Chuang-tzu replied: Not so. At first, when she died, how is it possible that I should not have felt grief? But I pondered over her beginning before she was born; not merely before she was born but when as yet there was no body; not merely was there no body but not even the vital spirit. Within an inchoate confusion there took place a transformation and there was vital spirit. The vital spirit was transformed and there came forth form, and with the transformation of form there was life. Now once again there is a transformation and she has died. What happened may be compared to the progression of the four seasons—spring, summer, autumn, winter. Now she is lying in peace in a large room. For me to follow after her weeping and wailing would be an indication that I have no thorough understanding of human destiny. So I stopped grieving.

Translated from the Chinese by D. H. Smith

INDEX OF POETS AND TRANSLATORS
(Translators are in italic. An asterisk signifies both poet and translator.)

INDEX OF TITLES

SOURCES & ACKNOWLEDGMENTS

Most of the poems in this anthology can be traced to a previously published New Directions edition. The year of publication is noted in parenthesis after each title. Poems from other sources are also listed below. Entries follow the order of the poems in the book. Thanks to all the poets, translators, agents, executors, and estates for their kind permission to reprint these poems and translations.

Gennady Aygi, "After Midnight – Snow Outside the Window" from *Field-Russia* (2007). Copyright © 2001 by Gennady Aygi. Translation copyright © 2007 by Peter France.

Tomas Tranströmer, "After Someone's Death" from *The Great Enigma: New Collected Poems* (2006). Copyright © 1966, 2006 by Tomas Tranströmer. Translation copyright © 2006 by Robin Fulton.

Coral Bracho, "That Space, That Garden" from *Firefly Under the Tongue: Selected Poems of Coral Bracho* (2008). Copyright © 2003 by Coral Bracho. Translation copyright © 2008 by Forrest Gander.

Dylan Thomas, "Grief Thief of Time" from *The Poems of Dylan Thomas* (1971, 2003). Copyright © 1953 by Dylan Thomas. Copyright © 1937, 1977 by the Trustees for the Copyrights of Dylan Thomas. Copyright © 2003 by New Directions.

Charles Tomlinson, "After a Death" from *Selected Poems: 1955–1997* (1997). Copyright © 1997 by Charles Tomlinson.

William Carlos Williams, "The Widow's Lament in Springtime" from *The Collected Poems of William Carlos Williams: Volume I 1909–1939* (1991). Originally published in *Sour Grapes* (The Four Seas Company: 1921). Copyright © 1921 by William Carlos Williams. Copyright © 2001 by the Estate of William Eric Williams and Paul H. Williams.

Alí Chumacero, "Widower's Monologue" from *The Collected Poems of William Carlos Williams: Volume II 1939–1962* (1991). Spanish original from Chumacero's *Palabras en reposa* (1956). Translation copyright © 2001 by the Estate of William Eric Williams and Paul H. Williams.

Inger Christensen, "Letter in April" from *Light, Grass, and Letter in April* (2011). Copyright © 1979 by Inger Christensen and Brøndums Forlag. Translation copyright © 2011 by Susanna Nied.

Gaius Valerius Catullus, "Two Translations of Poem 101" from *Nox* (2010) by Anne Carson and *Anew: Complete Shorter Poetry* (2011) by Louis Zukofsky. Copyright © 2010 by Anne Carson. Copyright © 1991, 2011 by Paul Zukofsky.

Jeffrey Yang is the author of the poetry books *Vanishing-Line* and *An Aquarium*. He is the translator of the Nobel Peace Prize Laureate Liu Xiaobo's *June Fourth Elegies* and Su Shi's *East Slope*, and the editor of *Birds, Beasts, and Seas: Nature Poems from New Directions*. He works as an editor at New Directions Publishing and New York Review Books.